Beneath the Sleepless
Tossing of the Planets
Selected Poems 1972–1989

Makoto Ōoka

Translated by
Janine Beichman

Preface by
Shuntarō Tanikawa

KURODAHAN PRESS
2018

Beneath the Sleepless Tossing of the Planets
Selected Poems 1972–1989

FG-JP0055L
ISBN: 978-4-902075-95-3

KURODAHAN PRESS
KURODAHAN.COM

Also by Ōoka Makoto

POETRY

A String Around Autumn: Selected Poems 1952–1980 (Translated by Ōoka Makoto with Thomas Fitzsimmons, Takako Lento, and Onuma Tadayoshi)

Elegy and Benediction: Selected Poems 1947–1989 (Translated by William I. Elliott and Kawamura Kazuo)

Linked Poems: Rocking Mirror Daybreak (With Thomas Fitzsimmons)

What the Kite Thinks: A Linked Poem (With Wing Tek Lum, Joseph Stanton, and Jean Yamasaki)

ESSAYS AND CRITICISM

The Colors of Poetry: Essays on Classic Japanese Verse (Translated by Takako U. Lento and Thomas V. Lento)

The Poetry and Poetics of Ancient Japan (Translated by Thomas Fitzsimmons)

ANTHOLOGIES

A Play of Mirrors: Eight Major Poets of Modern Japan (Translated by Ōoka Makoto, Thomas Fitzsimmons, and others)

A Poet's Anthology: The Range of Japanese Poetry (Translated by Janine Beichman)

Oriori no uta/Poems for All Seasons (Translated by Janine Beichman)

Love Songs from the Man'yōshū: Selections from a Japanese Classic (Translated by Ian Hideo Levy)

Poems for All Seasons: An Anthology of Japanese Poetry from Ancient Times to the Present (Translated by Janine Beichman)

101 Modern Japanese Poems (Translated by Paul McCarthy)

ŌOKA MAKOTO (1931-2017) was the premier poet and critic of his generation in Japan. Born in Mishima, a small city near Mt. Fuji, Ōoka began writing poetry in his teens. By the time he was twenty-five, his first books—one of poems and one of criticism—established him as a spokesman for contemporary poets. He often visited Europe, Asia, and the United States, lecturing and giving readings at the Collège de France, Harvard, Columbia, and Princeton Universities, as well as many literary festivals. His pioneering experiments with *renshi* or modern linked verse brought him into contact with poets around the world. President of Japan P.E.N. Club from 1989 to 1993, he was also a prolific translator who helped introduce to Japan modern poets such as Paul Éluard, André Breton, and John Ashbery. For almost three decades, Ōoka's daily column "Poems for All Seasons" ran on the front page of the *Asahi* newspaper, and through it poetry entered the daily lives of millions of readers in Japan. Ōoka's works have also been translated into Chinese, Dutch, Estonian, Finnish, French, German, Korean, Macedonian, and Spanish.

JANINE BEICHMAN (PhD, Columbia University) is author of biographies of the poets Masaoka Shiki and Yosano Akiko, and translator of Ōoka Makoto's *Poems for All Seasons/Oriori no Uta: An Anthology of Japanese Poetry from Earliest Times to the Present*. Her Noh play *Drifting Fires* was translated into Japanese by Ōoka Makoto. She is a judge for the JLPP Translation Competition of the Agency for Cultural Affairs of Japan and is a recipient of grants from the National Endowment for the Arts and the PEN America/Heim Translation Fund.

MICHELLE ZACHARIAS is a prize-winning artist who has exhibited widely in Japan and Canada and whose work can be found in private and corporate collections worldwide. She is an analogue artist in a digital age, specializing in etchings and colored pencil work. Being on the outside is no problem, since she is tall enough to stand on her toes and peek inside.
More of her work can be seen at http://www.mzacharias.com

Photo: Iwamoto Keiji

Ōoka Makoto in 2009.

Contents

from ***In Blackest Night, the Vacuum Cleaner of Heaven Is Full Upon Us*** (1987)

from ***Messages to the Waters of My Hometown*** (1989)

Japanese Names

In this book, Japanese names are given in traditional order, surname first, except for the cover and title page, where they are given in Western order for the convenience of libraries and booksellers.

"Ōoka" is pronounced with a doubled "o" followed by a single "o", like "OH-oka."

Preface

Ōoka Makoto was a brilliant critic, but—and I count it as one of his virtues—he was not an intellectual. I use the word as Paul Johnson does in his book *Intellectuals*, to mean someone who has forgotten that human beings are more important than ideas.

And yet this does not mean that human beings were all that Ōoka saw. As he wrote in "Back in Tokyo:"

> *But it's tiring, it really is*
> *this having a human face all the time*
> *And it's tiring*
> *to see nothing but human faces too*
> *In a crowded train*
> *one face like a starry sky*
> *or eyes like the ocean*
> *and a secret yearning fills me*

In these lines, Ōoka is placing human beings within the context of the universe; but there is no flight to abstraction, for he knows, in the deepest of senses, that human beings exist within the concrete reality of nature and the cosmos.

In the poems you will find in this volume, it is not difficult to see traces of the surrealist influence that colored Ōoka's youth. But Ōoka was never a blind worshipper of anything imported. For him, the attraction of surrealism lay not only in a personal affinity, but also in surrealism's resonance with the dominant pantheism at the heart of the traditional Japanese sensibility. Ōoka was deeply acquainted with this sensibility because of his thorough knowledge of classical Japanese literature. He was convinced that only when you approach phenomena from two opposite sides can you get a glimpse of the entirety, and that was always his method both in his poetry and in his criticism. One senses this even in the title of *Sad Songs and Blessings*, one of the books of poetry represented in this volume. It is clear even in these startling lines from "All about the Wind:"

> *A stream gives stones an enema.*
> *The sphincters of the pebbles quiver.*
> *Anguished quivering of the pebbles' flesh.*

Here stone and stream exist in a relationship of mutuality. The unexpected combination of the words "pebble" and "sphincter" may seem surrealistic but it was a conscious choice, not something that emerged unconsciously as in surrealism. Nor is it metaphorical, although it may sound like a metaphor. The existence of a sphincter in a stone is, rather, taken as fact. To the ancient Japanese, a stone may have been a god's dwelling place, but what Ōoka sees in a stone is neither divine nor sacred, but fleshly. Flesh is all, according to him, and still it is connected to spirit.

Rather than pantheism, the undercurrent of Ōoka's poetry is what, if there can be such a word, I would call paneroticism, and it is that which saves him from the abyss of abstraction. Ōoka, was, I am certain, aiming at a different wisdom than that of intellectuals when he wrote these lines:

> *Don't dwell on insignificant things.*
> *What you can see is endless,*
> *With your two eyes,*
> *With your one body.*
> *Don't indulge in speculation.*
> *Within you is the infinite.*

Tanikawa Shuntarō

Translator's Introduction

The Japanese treasure their writers, especially their poets, but the Ōoka Makoto Kotoba-kan— the Ōoka Makoto Museum of Words— stood out even in Japan for the beauty of its contemporary design and its seamless blend of poetry and art. When the museum opened in 2009 in Mishima, the city of Ōoka's birth, the center of the main exhibition room on the second floor was dominated by a circle of translucent silken banners dangling from the ceiling like long pale leaves, their tips hovering over the blond wood floor. Each was figured in soft gold lines that spelled out words from the ancient poets who appeared in Ōoka's long-running column *Poems for All Seasons*; viewers were meant to make a circuit through them, reading as they walked. In a corner of the large room, stood a replica of the study where Ōoka wrote his poems and criticism, complete with the homely detail of a sweater on the back of his chair. Small display cases on the perimeter of the room displayed his poetry notebooks and other memorabilia from childhood on. The walls held photographs of Ōoka with his wife (the playwright Fukase Saki) and his many friends and collaborators in the arts as well as a number of the works they had made, some of them with Ōoka. More than a museum dedicated to a single poet, it was a compendium of a world.

At the museum's last exhibition in its original space in 2017, the sides of the room were lined with wall pockets holding multiple copies of Ōoka's poems printed on thick cream-colored paper. In a gesture typical of Ōoka, who used to give away dozens of his new books to his friends, the museum visitors were invited to take the poems home with them. Meanwhile, the silken banners hanging down in the central space had been removed. Instead of being reimagined for the eye, Ōoka's work was now reinvented for the ear. This time it was not the ancient poets, but Ōoka's own poetry that was on display. In the center space, dark metal cylinders, open at the top, rose here and there from the light-colored floor. If you bent your ear to them, Ōoka's voice, recorded reading his own poems, could be heard, as if from the bottom of a well. Ironically, Ōoka himself, who had been seriously ill for some time, was by then unable to speak. That knowledge was not yet public but for the friends who knew the experience was poignant.

In 2014, a group of students, friends, and distinguished literary figures came together to create the Ōoka Makoto Society (Ōoka Makoto Kenkyūkai). Then, in 2016, Ōoka's wife, Fukase Saki, had the idea for a new *Ōoka Makoto: Self-selected Poems (Jisen Ōoka Makoto Shishū)*. Sitting alone with him, a mute audience of one, she read aloud every poem he had published, one by one. If he nodded yes, the poem went in, and if no, it was put aside. The result was a paperback volume of 125 poems, making his work accessible to a new audience, and with a thoughtful and detailed afterword by the critic Miura Masashi. In the year or so before he died, several previously published volumes of Ōoka's work gained new lives when they were reissued in the same kind of inexpensive paperback editions with new afterwords. In this group were Ōoka's magnum opus as a critic, *The Banquet and the Solitary Mind (Utage to Koshin*, originally published 1978), and two annotated volumes of *Poems for All Seasons (Oriori no uta*, originally published 1980 on). Looking back on this burst of activity, it almost seems that as Ōoka's body faded, his mind and spirit were bodied forth in new manifestations.

This new edition can be seen as one of these new manifestations. Now that we know there will be no more new poems by Ōoka Makoto, I felt the ones we had tugging at me, as if they were asking to be heard once more.

What has changed in this new edition? Major additions and revisions, as described below, were made in the material surrounding the poems, but little was changed in the translations themselves. I made a few changes in phrasing, one change in title, and corrected a few dates, but that was all. After all, the translations had been vetted by Ōoka himself, who read everything with a sharp eye, honed by his years of reading English poetry in the original. When our labors were almost done, Donald Keene kindly read the entire translation, comparing it to the original Japanese, and gave it his blessing too. There is no such thing as a perfect translation and surely there are many points to argue with, but there did not seem much point in trying to better what had resulted from the efforts of the three of us.

Certain departures from the original words were made at Ōoka's suggestion. For example, in "All about the Wind, " the line "I could make the ocean fit into a buttercup!" is a faithful translation of a new line that Ōoka added to the poem during the process of translation and will not be found in any of the published Japanese versions. In other cases, Ōoka changed a title to make it sound better in English. "Betsu no hi: Echizen de kani wo mita" (別の日 越前で蟹を見た) became, for this book, "Kani no hanashi" (蟹の話), or "Crab Talk."

Looking back now, I see that were other deviations that came from my efforts to restore what I felt slipping away as the poem moved from the language of its birth into a new world. Almost all of these centered around how I chose to paint the words on the page, that is, the spatial arrangement of words. Visual patterns can make up for some of what is inevitably lost in translation, and so can the sonic effects that line breaks and indents suggest to the ear. These are the things I had in mind when I indented lines to set them off, as in "Back in Tokyo" and "Poem for My Children," or when I broke longer lines up into shorter ones, as in the closing sections of "Chōfu I" and "Chōfu IV." Then there is "Life Story," where a word repeated in the Japanese is omitted in the English, and the words are now arranged on the page so that the one appearance does double duty. I aimed for fidelity to the original, but I use the word in both the narrow sense of being faithful to the literal meaning and the wider sense of being faithful to the spirit and the overall effect.

Ōoka's father was a tanka poet, but from early on Ōoka had a passion for French surrealism and its predecessors. The quintessential image he retained of himself from his college days was of sitting at a desk with the *Shinkokinshū* on one side and Baudelaire on the other. Thoroughly at home in the classical language of Japanese poetry, Ōoka invented a way of writing in modern colloquial Japanese that has the simplicity, succinctness, and elegance of the classical and sometimes even its underlying meter. He was able to fit the contours of everyday speech to those of classical poetry, and then suffuse the whole with a kind of surreal imagery. The result is a style that combines melodic sweetness and hard-cut brilliance. The most difficult part of translating these poems was to find a diction and tone as colloquial and yet as sparse and elegant as the originals. Some poets have a strangely intimate relationship to words, and not just to words in general, but to those of their own language. Ōoka Makoto was such a poet. He wrote in the presence of the entire Japanese language, past and present. (I borrow the phrase, *mutatis mutandis*, from Italo Calvino's description of Tommaso Landolfi.)

While the translations are mostly unchanged, in this new edition there are changes in the material that surrounds them. The major ones are that I revised my translation of Tanikawa Shuntarō's Preface and rewrote my own Translator's Note, in the process retitling it Translator's Introduction. There are also photographs and illustrations, new cover art, and the original Japanese texts of the poems.

My way of reading Ōoka's poems has also changed. When I was in the throes of translating, neither Ōoka nor I had time or even the desire to talk about interpretations of his poems except in a narrow sense. But after Ōoka died, I realized there was someone near him who could shed light on his motives and meanings. That was his wife, Fukase Saki, to whom he was so close.

"Song of the Nuclear Submarine *Thresher*, Its Sexual Sea Passage and Suicide" is based on the disappearance of the United States Navy's nuclear submarine USS Thresher in 1963. This incident is now almost forgotten but at the time Ōoka wrote the poem, when nuclear power was a topic of vital interest in the Cold War, it was comparable in impact to the 1986 space shuttle Challenger disaster. Without recourse to a dictionary, most English speakers might not realize that "Thresher" refers to the deadly "thresher shark," and not the agricultural tool. The situation is different in Japanese, for the Japanese word used in the title, *onagazame*, literally, "long-tailed shark," is crystal clear. This makes the personification of the submarine in Ōoka's poem perfectly natural.

Ōoka had expressed some unease when I wanted to include this poem in the collection as we were preparing the first edition, and late in 2017, when I was able to examine his poetry notebooks, I was fascinated to see that the draft of it in his notebook (see page 106) showed more evidence of revision than was usual for him. From other things I knew about Ōoka, I felt that he disliked politicizing literature in any way, whether for the left or the right, and I took his reluctance to have the poem translated as well as the evidence of revision as possibly connected to this concern.

One night in 2017, after Ōoka's death, I asked Fukase Saki if I was right that this poem was not meant to be an anti-nuclear or even an anti-American protest. Yes, she agreed, and added almost casually, "It's a *chinkon*," a poem to pacify the dead, to quiet their unsettled spirits. The word impressed me because until then I had only heard it applied to the elegies of Kakinomoto Hitomaro, the great court poet of the eighth century. I suddenly realized that the many poems Ōoka had written about friends on their death were *chinkon* too and that there were a large number of such poems in his oeuvre. To write modern *chinkon* poems for the dead may be something that only a poet with his strong ties to both the ancient and the contemporary could do.

The Thresher's loss was news around the world and led to a naval court of inquiry, but the mystery of its disappearance was never solved.[1] Some of the details (the yellow and white gloves, the fragments of cork, testimony) Ōoka mentions are taken from the published investigative reports, but the personified description of the sexualized submarine and the possibility that the sinking was suicidal are invented. The crux of the poem is the possible suicide of this instrument of destruction, shading into the prophetic fear that our own instruments of destruction will in the end destroy us. But the poem is framed by the motif, at both beginning and end, of the love between parent and child.

"Incantation," as performed by the magnificent Shiraishi Kayoko, was written as the opening speech of Ōoka's adaptation for the Waseda Shōgekijō of Euripides' *The Trojan Women*. There the dead, although not named, were understood to be the dead in the Trojan War, but on its own in the poetry collection, given that the particulars of who died are left blank, the poem becomes a poem for the dead of all times and places.

"Speak Please, I Beg You," is not explicitly identified as being about those who died in the bombings of Hiroshima and Nagasaki, but the details of the narration make clear that it is for them. Others have added the dedication to the victims that one sometimes sees when it is reprinted, but I feel that Ōoka would have resisted this as too specific. He grieved for the victims of the nuclear blast, but he also grieved for the crew of the Thresher. He grieved for human beings regardless of their nationality.

The poems for the dead are rooted in historical fact, but at the same time contain large elements of fantasy. They are analogous to a historical novel in which the author makes up details, dialogue, and even the characters' inner thoughts in order to convey an atmosphere and the sense of a time and place. Ōoka created a genre similar to the historical novel, blending fiction and fact. If one considers ancient epics like the *Odyssey* or the *Tale of the Heike*, and even many sacred texts (the Bible, the *Nihongi*), this seems part of an age-old tradition of transmitting the memory of historical events by retelling them as narrative poetry. Centuries from now, when the original historical materials are lost, they might even become legends or myths. I believe they are an important

---

1 John Bentley, *The Thresher Disaster: The Most Tragic Dive in Submarine History*, Doubleday, 1975.

part of Ōoka's oeuvre and significant works in the history of modern Japanese poetry.

Another kind of poem that struck me as I was preparing this new edition was Ōoka's eco-poems—written, it must be said, when there was not even such a word. Here belong "Crab Talk," "Insect's Dreams," "Chōfu IV." Then there are the poems about poetry, like "What is Poetry?" and the philosophical poems, like "Valley Stream Reflects the Mountain Light," and "In the Style of Goethe." And the love poems, the most famous of which is "Saki's Numazu."

Ōoka used the word "love" sparingly in his poetry. But all his poems are, in a sense, about love of different kinds and forms—for family, friends, the earth, for human beings alive and dead. To talk about love and nothing but love and yet rarely use the word: that may be what we remember him for best.

Janine Beichman
Tsukuba, September 2018

Acknowledgments

Rereading the translations as I prepared this new edition brought back the original excitement of making them, and the memory of how much I owed, and still owe, to Ōoka Makoto. Translating a poet who was such an enthusiastic and helpful collaborator was a tremendous pleasure and at the same time a formative experience for me as a translator. In many ways, Ōoka Makoto was my teacher.

In the acknowledgments for the first edition, I thanked those besides the author who read and commented on the translations and I am still very grateful to them: Carroll Aikins Beichman (now sadly deceased), Phyllis Birnbaum, Donald Keene, Aya Yamamoto, Miyabi (Abbie) Yamamoto, and Takeo Yamamoto.

In preparing this new edition, I incurred new and happy debts. Fukase Saki (Ōoka Kaneko) graciously granted permission to use the illustrative material, and with her deep and instinctive comprehension of her life companion's work, brought clarity and purpose to the project. I am tremendously grateful for her counsel. The skilled and supportive staff of the Ōoka Makoto Kotoba-kan, especially its director Iwamoto Keiji and the curators Nakamura Shōko and Ogawa Yuriko, went all out to locate and digitize the materials I needed among the massive holdings of the museum. Ochi Junko of the Ōoka Makoto Kenkyūkai generously shared materials she had digitized herself. Others who generously provided support and counsel include Jay Beichman, Phyllis Birnbaum (again), Edward Marx, Miura Masashi, Oda Yasuyuki, Paul Rossiter, John Solt, and Takeo Yamamoto (again), as well as the members of the Translators (Japanese <-> English) Facebook group who weighed in on how to explain the pronunciation of Ōoka Makoto's surname and other matters. And a special thanks to Edward Lipsett, for keeping the pleasure in it all. Any infelicities or inaccuracies that remain are of course my own responsibility.

These poems to which I have given birth have given birth to me.
Epilogue—*Aquapolis, Invisible Town*

from *A Perspective Diagram of Summer*

(1972)

透視図法―夏のための

Daybreak Leaf Alive
Akatsuki Happa ga Ikite iru

Somehow there was
a cool rain bathing
the fruit's insides
that dawn

The leek and the tofu
turned into beads of fragrant scent,
vying in lightness with the light
And also the waves of the woman's robe,
carelessly flung on the floor

Hand resting on the chilly phone,
she was staring at the sand
as it began to lighten
Even gulls melted into the hush,
the tide heavy at dawn

Awake
the whole night through,
was there a border for them
between today and yesterday?

The two were a cave that held the heavens,
were a cosmic mandala that waxed full there

And yet somehow
the woman
was a forest of fragrance,
was the light of dawn,
running to the dawn's own depths

I saw a single leaf
go mad with joy at the sound
of a waterfall high in the blue sky

Somehow the leaf
was taking a leisurely spin
around the edge of a field

Somehow
that single leaf's words
went on
forever

and they were mine

A Perspective Diagram of Summer

Tōshizuhō—Natsu no Tame no

The room is so full of pillars, it looks like a forest.

I sense that a corridor runs around it, but my eyes are drawn not to the perimeter but to the center of the room, so I am not sure just how wide the corridor is.

Shelves like horizontally spreading wings fill the room. They are the soft respiratory organs of mossy stone ledges, and are equipped with lips. This suggests that the room might be behind the pool at the base of a waterfall. But there is a thick gray carpet on the shelves, which I see, going closer, is a solid layer of dust.

I feel myself mumbling, "I didn't know that dust was this full of the mouse's roar." Just then a small woman with a large pipe in her mouth appears, lashing her sinuous electric ray tail back and forth like a whip.

"I'd like to go in some direction other than the usual four, but from the wall of what art museum should I sally forth?" she asks.

And answering her own question,

"It's in my bookshelf, third shelf from the top."

She goes on,

"What makes you say, my sweet, that Babylon's been destroyed, when it's just in the middle of being built."

And answering her own question,

"But it's true, I'm sure. I saw it myself, when the Security Pact was being washed away downriver."

She turns towards me, and it is fierce-looking Denise, the art dealer who years ago said "Let me make you a little museum," gave me several beautiful lithographs and then shook my hand like a man. Her shining hair is divided into two shell-shaped sections, black as obsidian, just as it had been then. So she had been wearing a wig, after all!

She offers me a transparent book. Its title, *Summer*, is thickly embossed in letters a hundred times bigger than the largest type. As I reach out for it, the book's four corners crumble to powder and blow away. I stare at her suspiciously and realize that this is not Denise: it is my own wife!

"What do you think you're doing riding around on a bike? Don't you realize that the words "tree of fire" are flickering on your hand?"

"The neighborhood kids couldn't find enough round stones in the woods to play kick the stone with so they've just made some balls out of air. A World's Fair is sure a busy place. Everyone's slurping up instant ramen."

"No, no you've got it all wrong! Ever seen a landscape by Constable? Know how every dewdrop on the grass has a lot of damselflies flitting about in it? And the whole Fair is wrapped up in their eyeballs, and you can see the underside of the asphalt there, like a droopy felt hat."

As I speak, I plunge my hand into the clouds which are rapidly closing in. Then a sudden electric discharge sends a fantastically pleasant shock through my whole body. I become a pillar of ascending air; but who are those cheerfully smiling people gathered in a knot on a hill? A woman's fleshy hips, turned sleek and trim, are the site of a row of beautiful horses galloping around and around in perfect synchrony.

"Kōjima Ōshi, Kōjima Ōshi"

Like the roving wooden clappers that warn against fire at night, a voice gradually approaches from beyond the horizon. It is calling my name. I find myself running towards it. I run over the horizon, heading for my friend's house, through a heavy rain mixed with lime from the stalactites in the Akiyoshidai Caves. But no matter how hard I look, my friend's face has no definite shape. "Kōjima Ōshi" is written on the house-sign in an exotic medley of kanji, the ones used by the monster who has inspired some of my most thrilling fantasies for years, so I realize that this is his house. But then I remember that the monster's name was actually Kōzuma and realize indignantly that the Kōjima Ōshi who was being called a little while ago and the Kōzuma I know have somehow become confused; and then I'm calling out "Ke-enji, Ke-enji!" across a crumbling bamboo hedge. After I've been calling for a while, a young boy appears from the crack between two sliding paper doors. He is riding on a white cloud and using both hands to unroll something that looks like a sutra scroll. He is a sleepy-eyed fellow I've never seen before, but I remember at once that his name is Kenji, and ask,

"Is your father back?"

His father has been gone for ten years. They say he went off to the war, but I don't know which one. The boy addresses me:

"I'm really in a fix because I don't have enough bamboo leaves. They're the best thing for polishing bird stomachs. Could you pick me some?"

The boy has a white beard as long as my arm. Of course, I am still in grade school, so my arm isn't that long, only about the same as a fully uncurled leaf of the wild ferns we like to pick on the dike. My arms full of wild ferns and bracken, I go with Kenji to the street corner where we like to hang out. There is a little tobacco shop there which has a scroll with a passage from the Lotus Sutra hanging on the wall just to the left as you go in, and right in front of it the comfortable cushion where the old woman who owned the store sat doing business all day. There is a small wooden drum, its top worn away, which I always longed to take to school and show off to everyone. The owner of the store was my grandmother. Next to the tobacco store was the Uchida Rice Store and next to that Okura-san's house, the one we always threw firecrackers at and ran away. Okura-san always burst out of the house barefoot, her hair a mess, and chased after us yelling "You little monsters!" Today something glitters in her hand as she pursues us. As I run frantically, I remember that Okura-san is schizophrenic. If she's schizoid, I'm okay. I realize that even if she sees me, she won't realize that I'm the one who threw the firecrackers. I turn back, a nonchalant look on my face. Okura-san runs up all out of breath, swinging the knife. The bottom of her kimono is hanging open and her shins and thighs are exposed. I hold my breath and slip by, purposely rubbing against her soiled kimono. At the corner of her eyes, I glimpse tears that look like they've been falling for many years, solidified now, dangling there like a string of beads. At that moment, my own face is reflected in my own eyes: it is the head of a huge black crow. Kenji is nowhere to be seen.

Cooling the container of the world, the wind blows violently. Deep in the forest, in that dark room, the black dust blows sideways with terrific force, scattering from the many gray shelves spread out like wings. But the beautiful woman standing at the center of the room remains, untouched by the wind's menace. I realize that this is because the thick, full hair that covers her from her neck to her breasts has miraculously become a shimmer of spring haze spiraling about her. I know she is my friend, but I can not for the life of me remember her name. Every second her face turns into someone else's.

The dust blows off the gray shelves and flies sideways with the force of a blizzard, preventing me from going near the beautiful snow maiden at its center. Then as I cover my nose with my hand and force myself to hold my breath, my retreating figure turns into the foreground and everything slides back into a deep perspective, seeming from where I stand beautifully, poignantly, transparent.

Dream of April 16, 1970

from *Beneath the Sleepless Tossing of the Planets*

(1975)

遊星の寝返りの下で

Incantation

Ju

The opening lines of Ōoka's adaptation of Euripides' The Trojan Women, *as performed by the Waseda Shogekijo Theatre.—Tr.*

Dead souls, live:
   in these arid stones
   and in the roots of distant trees
If colors,
   be the color of dawn
   the lustrous pearl of spilt tears
Dead souls, live:
   simultaneously on all
   the thousand peaks of this planet
   with its two frozen poles
If feet,
   be a whirlwind of hyenas
   ostriches, ferocious cobras
Dead souls, depart and live:
   in the still dark pools
   at the far limits of light
If hands,
   be the maelstroms oceans breed
   the nimbleness of a girl's fingers
   stitching
Dead souls, live:
   leaving no footprints behind
   following the pure sky path
   reclining on its golden waves
If song,
   be the tune of an army travelling forever
   love songs
   the coolness of the earthworm's eternal song
Dead souls, forsake us
   who live in swamps shut off from the sun
   become fruit that stings the tongue
   return to life
And if you are breath, then be
   the world's first and last,

a woman's delicate sigh,
the holy fire of the demon air,
and return to life
return to life
Return to life

Dead souls!

Her Fragrant Flesh, or How I Met a Madwoman
Kanojo no Kaoru Nikutai, Mata wa Watakushi no Deatta Kyōjo

On an evening that made me think of the faint light given off by air trapped underwater in frozen skeins of blanket weed, I came across a woman. She was alone.

She looked like a madwoman, but as she approached a tombstone, the stone, inspired, broke into speech.

In a low voice, it explained that the woman was clairvoyant and a sorceress. Everyone knows that those with the power of second sight have always been forced to take on the outer lineaments of the mad, but still it pained me to see how her youthful face quivered with the ripples of a fourth-dimensional sexual allure.

The wind blew anxiety towards us.

The flutter of birds' wings was filled with longing.

The water was a bed where eternal life and death flowed into one another. An endless roar echoed from that couch of love. It was a giant potter's wheel that changed the autumn leaves, the blue sky, and flames to a roar.

"Are you no more than meaning? Or are you a great symbol? Reply!"

I could not tell if the question came from the madwoman or the tombstone, but I heard myself answering:

"I am the lid on top of memory. Unto you I say: I exist only in order to be dug up and removed. But I am also the air that looks up in surprise from beneath the lid at myself become a lid. And I am that air's memory. Do I then exist?"

"No, you're wrong. You are not a lid. You are entombed alive in memories, though, a puerile old man. You must make your blood flow in the streets. When the blood rushes out, when thorns of pain sprout on your whole body, when you lay yourself down on those thorns, then for the first time, you will know that you are flesh, nothing more and nothing less. Pain will become your words, tears your meaning. Without this, your words will not weigh even sixty kilograms. Look at you now, light as a snowflake!"

The chilly wind hurt my ears. I was flying somewhere high, held up by her. Become time within a lump of flesh, I bobbed lightly in empty space.

"Look!"

She pointed to a sharp arrow aimed at a deep eddy of intoxication whirling in space. Letters of light spelled out *pleasure* and trembled on its tip. Suddenly, I felt the glow of lust burn my body and moaned.

"Words are the real shape of deeds, you know. Hey, look at that!"

Shadowy letters lay where she pointed. They spelled out *knowledge.* In an instant my eyes swept from the bottom of the River Styx to the construction of an electronic brain.

"Knowledge and pleasure are connected by the tunnel of intuition. Mozart had the power to visualize completely the music he was about to write in transparent, three-dimensional form. To him, intuition was knowledge, and also pleasure. I know, because I lived inside his brain. The faculty of intuition works through the lacerated wounds of knowledge, and of pleasure. Have you ever known anything as pleasurable as being wounded?"

I tried to raise my voice in surprise, but her hand deftly erased the word *knowledge* as it lay before me. I had a splitting headache but it was completely different from the shock of intuition. I felt tears begin to ooze out on to my skin and freeze.

"Look!"

She pointed towards a mountain of garbage which moved continuously, as though churning up space. It was an awe-inspiring tower of blood, rotten things, the wreckage of all sorts of weapons, and odds and ends of human bodies, animals and plants. There was no arrow or letters.

"Human beings can't resist trying to name this mountain of garbage. There's something in garbage that brings out the naming lust. Some foolish man looked at this mountain and cried *It's a mountain of wealth.* In his own society, he passed for a very rich man. Another one called it *Belief.* And there was another who said *It's the very shape of revolution,* and still another who said *It's the pagoda of life.* And of course there were those who called it *Death* and *Love.* And then the honest man who could only say *It's a mountain of garbage!.* So many, many men tried to discover in this mountain the little desires and the big fears they felt about life. But the only one who heard them all was me.—Well now, what's your choice?"

I was listening to the woman's words as I flew along in her embrace. Her breast was broad and deep, and suddenly I yelled out in jealousy,

"Have you flown through the sky embracing all those men?!"

"So you've fallen in love with me, too!"

She kissed the nape of my neck tenderly. Suddenly, deep lines appeared at the corners of her eyes and I felt myself enfolded even more deeply into her breast. Her kiss sent a chill through my blood as if I'd been pierced by a needle of ice. I screamed in ecstasy.

"You're crazy. A madwoman, a witch!"

"Poor thing. Some of the young ones really fall in love with me. They have the illusion they're flying through the air wrapped in my embrace. I've been given the power of second sight, but I can't help men like that. Because if they really shared my bed, they would go mad."

But I was shouting in delirium.

"What an acute angle of the air! What a journey of revelation! What a violent embrace!"

Then a mass of people gathered around me, staring at me and smirking.

I was standing on earth stark naked, covered all over with dew from the dawn fields. I examined my body and saw that one part of it was violently excited and pointing up into space.

Beyond the wall of people, the vista of a dusty city unfolded, a highway snaked along, businesses spread out, and a poster advertising the complete works of Baudelaire flapped against the wall of an office building.

I screamed out,

"Listen to me! Tell me your name!"

The human wall burst into laughter and crumbled away. The woman whispered in my ear.

"Some people called me poetry. But that was in very ancient times. The moderns call me by various exaggerated names. But no one has ever made me a woman. There were some who slept with me, but they all went mad or became invalids and could never be men to me again. From that instant, they became part of me, so I ended up always sleeping with myself. I guess I'll have to endure this thirst forever, while those called poets will know only their unrequited love. I want real blood, my own, to flow in the streets. I want to become meaning heavy as the body. I want to make tears, decay and garbage my own, my own!"

II

I was so deeply absorbed in my own vision that I had even forgotten my own name. I felt sight turn suddenly to blindness, but my hearing became exquisitely sharp even at the deepest level. Hearing is a nocturnal sense. I was a single heavenly body that held all of night within.

Pink Eye Dissected

Crocodile Tears Given To Quantitative Analysis

A Stumbling Coral Reef
Earthen Wall Breathing In And Out
Volcanos Slumber On
Sloping Spring And Plum Blossoms
Bell Chimes Vaporize
Shepherd's Whistle Crystallizes
Ship's Carpenter Becomes A Whirlpool And Runs Away
An Adiabatic Name

One after another, words welled up and images gushed forth from the words and together they undulated in waves, forming a single shape, and this shape gradually began to take form as me.

The sun was the honey of the gods. With the magnificent solemnity of the day heaven and earth were created, honey flowed deep in the sky. The sky was a beehive. The wind was the eggs of shining bees that followed a fixed course from this hive then scattered in all directions. I follow it and scattered in all directions, too.

Empedocles spoke on Mt. Empedocles: "The power of Love and Hate is the source of both the coming together and going apart of fire, water, air and earth. In the distant future, our species will repeat many different interpretations of this fact, only to end in darkness."

However, atoms do not like to change form and they all came together in a circle in the shape of the words "Lord, be by my side as evening falls" and snuggled up to each other.

A non-compressible fluid turned into a pole of light and gave off a roar as it bumped against the girders of a bridge in the sky. To the rhythm of that drum, a girl played a flute cut from the shinbone of a bull, and by a desolate lake a boy played another made from a reed. On two shores 1,000 kilometers apart, they were about to perform the first music to sound through the world. Everything was moving quickly, with the magnificent solemnity of the day heaven and earth were created.

"You are now lying within my womb for the first time. But I won't give birth to you. I can't, because I've given birth to you already."

It was her voice again. I said,

"Why do I need to be born at this late date? I'm fully alive in this ecstatic moment of the world's birth! O nature, how lovely this fresh morning when the stars begin to fall!"

The woman tittered. Her laughter made her visible to me. Her beautiful face, of indeterminate age, appeared before me.

"Ecstasy? A fresh morning?"

Her laughter seemed to dissolve the preservatives within me at once. My heart shrank. Within that high-pressure pain, I realized that I was trapped in myself, fated to decay. Anger washed over me, and I was overcome by a fit of trembling.

"O, fountain! If I knew such bliss, then why, why did I feel that my body had been shaped into a miniaturized constant number? Oh continent of lost harmonies, within my flesh...!"

The woman gazed fixedly at me.

"My energy is negative."

She certainly seemed to be murmuring that, but at that very instant, she disappeared.

"Wait! That's not true. It's you who are the image! It's you who are poetry! I know you're not inside me! But many different radiations contain you! Unique and constant existence! Living without being born, discovered without being sought, the true shape of my own shadow! I am included in you and so include you! Orbit of transcendent meaning, naked rose! My bee-honey! Wait!"

Then I noticed that I had become an ant, and was gathering sap from the trees by a river outside a large city.

Now that I was an insect, it was clear that most of the world was made of antennae. My food was bad, my labor constant. The deafening sounds coming from the direction in which I turned my antennae completely muffled sounds from elsewhere. This made me unconsciously revolve my antennae, in order to gauge the vibrations and direction of the sounds.

"I've turned into radar. But there's a blind spot when I revolve. My own body keeps me from turning my antennae towards my head and lower torso. If an enemy appears, it will be from directly beneath me."

Even though I constantly changed position, I was overcome with anxiety and turned my steps toward the maze of the city streets, the dewy plateaus, and the sandy lowlands. My food was bad, my labor constant.

"My poems are the naked body of electric waves!"

"My poems are a cloud chamber for antenna!"

The grass-lark was singing in its glass box in the sky. The stars were tossing uncomfortably in their sleep, and their blood leaked out like light from earthly gems. Tremendous hands reached vertically down as though to grab something and tangled at the tips, in fierce battle. The blood of a broken finger ran through its own promontory pulling a vein of water behind, and was taken up by the beehive of the sky. And what a miracle of rotation it was that the sky did not become a sea of blood but still shone with the iridescence of honey.

The sky was a cheerful phenomenon.

"You are living for one more minute, which stretches to eternity. No matter how late it gets, it's always that final minute. Can you puncture your labor, and vaporize time? Can you pierce your meditation and evaporate time?"

After the voice, the woman's face emerged, a sphere lit by an inner light. It was a planet and had a tremendous, detailed shadow on its surface. Veiled in a light mist like the delicate green epidermis of a tree after its bark has been peeled away, it drifted before me, approached, then suddenly disappeared. A terrible pain assaulted me, and I saw my antennae convulse and catch fire. My six legs fell every which way, and became food for the other ants to drag away. My thin-waisted thorax, shining like a black diamond, slowly swelled up as my blood vessels quietly pulsed, and hair began to grow on my body. I was dyed with blood.

And now I became human and screamed in pain:

"What a sharp angle of the air! What a journey of revelation! What a violent embrace!"

But—and I'm sure I was not mistaken—the voice was not mine. It was *her* voice, welling up from within mine!

"Where are you? Where are you?"

No reply. But I felt something glued tightly to the inner surface of my skin. It made the fish and birds within me sleep like fragrant stones. The sun within turned to flowing honey.

"See, didn't I tell you I was negative energy?"

It could have been the murmurings of insect larvae on the wind as they parted from their nest in the sky. I shrieked,

"Wait! Stop! You beautiful moment! You beautiful, crazy woman!"

Then a mass of people gathered around me, staring at me and smirking.

There I was, standing on earth stark naked, covered all over with dew from the dawn fields. I looked down at my body. My flesh had become a gently sloping hill melting into the golden air of dawn.

Beyond the wall of people, the vista of a dusty city unfolded, a highway snaked along, businesses spread out, and a poster advertising the complete works of Baudelaire flapped against the wall of an office building.

I thought I had seen this scene somewhere before, but I couldn't be sure.

I screamed out,
"Listen to me! Tell me your name!"
The human wall burst into laughter and crumbled away.
I can not hear the woman's murmurs or her laughter. But feeling that everything is moving quickly with the magnificent solemnity of the day heaven and earth were formed, I begin to walk towards the ruined city.

Speak Please   I Beg You
Itte kudasai   dō ka

He said:
Let living things be born without end
in the waters
Let birds fly without end
in the blue sky over earth

He made
the giant fish
and all the creatures that breed
in the waters
as groups of
        like and like,
and He made
all the winged birds
as groups of
        like and like,
and slowly waved His hand
in blessing
        to the edge of night

Stars fell glittering from His fingers
and from the Milky Way to my small shack
His voice rang out

        Peace on Earth
        Joy to the World

Help me please   I beg you
Even sunset does not want to live
in a forest of bones   in a forest of bones I wander
in search of a bit of blue sky
and I've found a bit of a tiny finger
Look
just look! It's
my sweetheart's pinky, that she cut off and gave me
and I sucked so small

He made people
in the spitting image of Himself
He blessed human beings and said

Be fruitful
Multiply

Through the rivers of Asia
the lakes of Europe
the canals of America
the waterfalls of Africa
human skin
flows,
        like cucumber peels

In faceless countries
faceless hands
count out coins damp with blood

He created
infinite time and finite time
infinite space and finite space
In only seven days
He completed the whole job
And then
He purified it all

Peace on Earth
Joy to the World

I was walking down a big stone street
and my feet gave off a dull light
I asked the way of a man in a ragged hat
and went on and on
but never arrived
"You know, back there I asked a man in a tattered jacket
for directions, but couldn't find the way"
"Oh, that must have been the fellow from the barbershop
next to the fountain, the one who died just like that
of the bug that was going around eight years ago"

My kind informant was,
said the grapevine, the mapmaker
who'd drowned in the river fifty years ago
No, I'm wrong—
One summer all of a sudden
a light 50,000 times brighter than the sun
flashed in the sky and
everyone without exception   in an instant
          moved to this town
There are no funerals and flowery wreaths
no voices of children at play
Everyone's walking like me now
just as they were then
like shadows on water
In this town even the human silhouettes burned into
stone steps take their constitutionals
The whole town's burned into
one of those black holes the universe has

Maybe I'll meet you
in that town someday
After all, it's the star
where we were born

Speak please   I beg you
     "You naughty child,
     you're dreaming
     again."

from *Sad Songs and Blessings*

(1976)

悲歌と祝禱

All About the Wind
Kaze no Setsu

The wind has neither seed nor stem. Unlike fruit it knows
  no completion.
I walk, and a wind rises at my feet. Only to suddenly disappear,
  a sigh. The true wind always rises far away, and vanishes
  there, too.
The wind has neither seed nor stem. Unlike fruit it knows
  no ripening.
Always somersaulting, always gliding, the wind is a transparent
  wayfarer bent on filling every gap.
Let's call it water, sent to the sky.

*
After rain. There are shallows.
I grope through a forest.
Colored birds breed. White sound penetrates the sky.
A stream gives stones an enema.
The sphincters of the pebbles quiver.
Anguished quivering of the pebbles' flesh.
When the wind trembles
the sun turns inside out and overflows the fields:
Now the eye can travel a thousand leagues in a twinkling.
The wind whispers in my ear,
"You know, if I just had the drugs that light does,
I could make the ocean fit into a buttercup"
Wind, sweet fool
You with your generous, two-timing heart!

*
A separate wind floats by.
Human whispers, that never ripened to proper words.
Speech like that
is all but dead—then why do I miss it so?

Isn't it because
the vapors whisper faintly through the nights
of careful ritual, piling up dew
thick on the hairs of each tree leaf?

Isn't it because
human beings induce the sap and whispers in the trees
by nightly swaying their neurons' tree-shaped nodes?

And isn't it because between them,
somersaulting, gliding, bent on filling
every gap, a transparent wayfarer
is stringing a net across the depths of space?

Dreaming Sam Francis
Samu Furanshisu wo Yumemiru

Day broke   and Sam Francis in the clouds
looked out   saw nothing like a cloud
No shadows, only waterdrops, everywhere a deluge

   "Ascetic, you have form! Seek
   the transcendent, which has none!
   Truth is formless"—
So spoke the whirlwind
All was whiteness floating

Sam watched mountains of massive clouds well up
from deep within his eyes

His fingertips gave off sparks but not electric ones
   "Artist, you have form! Seize
   mystery, which has none!
   Clouds are formless"—
So spoke Sam's lips to Sam

What receded was more richly shadowed
than what was coming near

Sam ran far off

Distance and nearness changed places
In the color wheel of the magnificent world
sunset merged with sunrise and embraced the darkness

In the dream of a Zen priest the beard of Socrates,
Sam's uncle, blinks wildly   swims away
its 10,000 dextrous hands paddling
10,000 dextrous hands paddling

Socrates' bestial laugh
crashes into the cosmic map
where Blake digs with his spade
and Sam stands bathed
in the sparks of his youth

The world a crackling maze
undulating invisible splashes
The quiet solitude of an imperial tomb
struck with wonder   soars majestically
Sensing which, the studio walls tremble
The white space of the canvas shines

Among colored shapes, Sam embraces
the warmest, softest things
a woman's spirit
in the shape of clouds
in the shape of foam
in the shape of a womb
The white space of the canvas shines

In the midst of a life lived among plastic and ammonia
Sam's flesh is shaken by metaphysical orgasms
sinks deep down

A lion sinks into thunder clouds
    bares its white teeth, a great rain
    bites into the shoulder of sleeping desire

Desire, love for the immortal
But "Eternity   is in love with the productions of time"
    so murmurs Blake
And now the paints the brushes burn bright
        as their life nears its end,
they radiate ecstasy
Sam radiates

California darkness gives off an orange glow
Sam's darkness gives off the light of human honey

Paintings are a message from beyond themselves

Sam is given messages from beyond himself

From beyond, the darkness   trembling in ecstasy
sinks eager fangs into Sam's paintings

from *Spring, to a Virgin*

(1978)

春

少女に

Fruits of Light
Hikari no Kudamono

The hemispheres of your chest
rest on my hands   far off on a distant sea

So heavy these fruits   made of light!
A thorn, you pierce the lining
of my insides   crawl within

Distance makes you
     overflow into me
Absence forces you
     to make a home inside my heart

Deep at night you became
eighty four thousand stars
pierced my dreams   passed through me

And I watched through the cracked glass
as the eighty four thousand stars
shot through you, and scattered you in bits across the sky

Insects' Dreams

Mushi no Yume

"That time I fell and got earth in my mouth,
it tasted awful, but the vegetables
and flowers born from the earth have a lot
of pipes that carry sweet dew, don't they?"

Child,
it's just as you say
Look out over the Musashi Plain—
See how the air is fluttering like a handkerchief?
Know how the earth looks dark and deep on winter evenings?
The grinder bug that jumped more brightly than music,
the water spider that swirled the cloudy water,
the long-horned beetle,
the ant-lion—
they've all gone quietly back
to the big cellar beneath the earth

Child,
because you are human,
don't forget,
even when you build a house of stone,
the insects sleeping under the earth,
their legs jerking now and then,
the long bibs of their dreams

Even they dream, you know—
technicolor dreams   of harvest
dreams like music   of water

Because you are human, you must not forget—
It isn't humans who give the pure sweet water
to the plants and flowers,
it is the hard dark tasteless
earth

Because you are human

from *Aquapolis, Invisible Town*

(1981)

水府　みえないまち

Chōfu I
Chōfu I

Chōfu is an area of Tokyo where the poet lived for several years.—Tr..

Living in a town,
I think about towns
    The one I live in, oddly enough,
    never comes to mind

Eyes and memory always veer off
to a different town—
    But it's not like longing
    for a different woman

Like the horsefly grazing among the dayflowers
and the shepherd's purse on the hill, then slowly drifting off
    into the distance,
        lost in the pleasure
           of flying itself,

so there, stumbling back from a tower that sways among clouds
then arriving, somehow, in another town, one
    wreathed in a separate air,
        is

           me

Chōfu IV

Chōfu IV

On a day near the end of March
toads well up in throngs
from the earth around the house
   hundreds awake
   from hibernation
   on the very same day
the scrawny males
riding the backs of the hefty females
sometimes an extra male holding on
for dear life, slipping down
then scrambling up again
   Until last year they descended upon
   the pond in the neighbor's garden
   hordes of them arriving in endless waves
Were the pond still there, they'd breed day and night
But the pond's dried up and
the nearest water is in the woods
   Yet still the toads sing on in praise of love
   They look dazed
   like "country gram and gramps off on a trip"
   as city folks like to say
But when they let loose
look out, you Mick Jaggers
Those fat bellies send the echoes far and wide
the very air vibrates
with their noisy, cheerful cries
   Croak your gurgly croaks, you common frogs
   Four or five days running
   the sky resonates day and night
   then all at once every voice stops dead
   Their duties fulfilled
   they reenter the earth and sleep until summer comes

When human eyes play lightly over the earth
the toads are curled up breathing
under the cherry trees over there

Above them
petals
s
  c
    a
    t
  t
e
r
 i
   n
    g

The Cliffs of London
Rondon Kengai

Vivienne Haigh-Wood,
dancer,
and Thomas Stearns Eliot,
poet,
married.

Soon Thomas published his maiden work,
The Love Song of J. Alfred Prufrock,
and achieved fame.

These lines for the hero,
a middle-aged prude, were a big hit:

"For I have known them all already, known them all –
Have known the evenings, mornings, afternoons,
I have measured out my life with coffee spoons"
Then Thomas wrote *The Waste Land*

and his reputation took off like lightning
jolting the peaks, flickering over the fields.
Standing in the wasted fields of modernity
Thomas thought he might become another Dante.

Vivienne
got sick,
her mind began to go,
16 years into marriage.

Eventually she entered a mental asylum,
lived there 16 years,
died.

The root of her sickness?
Even the gods don't know.
But I am one who
believes from the depths of my being,
with deep respect,

that people can go mad from love.

Women who go mad from love shred up poems,
leave for a higher realm from which
they shed a far disdain on poets.

I don't know if Vivienne
was one of them or not, but
I know, with deep respect,
that there are such women.

A year after his wife's death
Thomas received the Nobel Prize.
17 years later
Thomas Stearns Eliot,
trailing the January mists of the Thames,
left for heaven.

Many obituaries and evaluations followed him,
but I read only one
very short one.
A journalist, speaking of the occasions
he and Eliot had shared, wrote:

"After Vivienne was institutionalized
in 1931
until her death
in 1947,
Eliot visited his wife without fail
every Thursday
for 16 years.
However,
she never knew
who her visitor was"

The journalist also related something
Eliot had said to him one day:

"I plunge into a word and
if I decide I like it,
I keep it to use one day.

I hung on to 'philogenitive' for a long time,
before I finally used it.

But there's one word
I've never been able to find
a use for: antelucan
If you like, I'll give it to you.
I know I'll never use it now;
It's too Miltonian"

antelucan: "before the dawn"

Envoy
    Words I haven't used yet

shin ni iru	Olympian art
kugo no tōne ya	distant strains of an ancient lute
akigumori	cloudy autumn sky

The poet Ōoka's "words I haven't used" form a haiku describing the poet Eliot's art.—Tr.

Saki's Numazu
Saki no Numazu

A memory of the time when Ōoka was a college student in Tokyo and his future wife Fukase Saki was recuperating from tuberculosis in her hometown of Numazu, the town in Shizuoka where they had first met. — Tr.

The sea that mirrors the sky
is a different sea from midnight
When you come into my thoughts
I lift myself on flames of snow
I dive through the sea, set
you, my moon, afloat
high in the sky

Your chest is heavy in my hands
The hundred kilometers between us
is my horizon, a tightrope I must cross
All night
I grope my way until, at the very end
in the exhaustion of early dawn
I finally knock on your door
The door of your lungs where T.B. lives

Leaves fall
The birds fly high
In the wintry field turned light our feet trace a path
The ants of pain are napping
Afraid of their awakening
still we trace a path for them
by ourselves

Look—
When the sea reflects the sky
each fish's eye
is framed in a golden sun
As they sink, the fishes nibble
at the seaweed with flat jaws and
fall asleep with eyes wide open
Like souls who suffer deeply, all unaware

Don't you see?
Standing next to us
are our doubles
fast asleep
Not knowing pain
they sleep

And so again and again
I lift myself on flames of snow
I dive through the sea, set
you, my moon, afloat
high in the sky beyond
the red sun of Numazu, distant home

Cerebropolis
Nōfu

—Leave tomorrow's wind to tomorrow, you say?

Something terrible was going to happen.
Every room in every house felt it.

Some people were already secretly building shelters.
Some had already drowned in the sewers, trying to escape.

From the town's first cell-room to its fourteen billionth,
shock and tension at the slightest change in wind pressure.

And yet the sounds of music echoed, and there was love.

Lovers walked together tenderly,
but they too held their breath and waited.

That voice for which everyone was waiting
was within each of them:

"Oh, let's just tear it all down already.
I want to breathe easy again. Easy."

To let it out:
That was the most terrifying
thing of all.

Rhymopolis
Infu

Fountain-head,
I tell you:
you are poetry
so don't
leak

Chōfu VIII
Chōfu VIII

To a certain matron

The heart rejoices at a good poem
no matter how hateful the person
who wrote it.

But in that small thing resides
the secret of poetry.

It's an insignificant secret, to be sure,
but it is undeniable however you try.

California: Unvoiced Harmonies
Kashū Mokkei

The mental counterpoint between Japan and America as the poet Ōoka travelled through the western United States in 1978 is echoed in the alternation between free verse and the brief tanka, a traditional Japanese form.—Tr.

The noisy rustle of withered magnolia leaves,
The slow scattering of crimson leaves deep at night,
Lower leaves so thick
You can't see an inch ahead—I forget those woods in Japan
Upon that other shore across the sky and
Pass through forests of aspens, leaves like gold.

    / aspens shine yellow
  on the red rock back of the canyon
  autumn shows itself

  / aspens are like gingkos
  their leaves are brittle
  their dry rustle disturbs the heart

"Don't dwell on insignificant things.
Don't indulge in speculation.
Only submit to the diversity of all there is to see.
Only be overcome.
And overcome.
Don't dwell on insignificant things.
Only pass them by.
And while passing,
Pay your respects to what you leave behind.
To what stays behind, pay your respects."

It was the wind over the pale waves of Fish Lake,
Silent at the end of the corridor of white-trunked aspens,
That spoke this to me.
It was mid-October, at the end of my journey.
The heat wave had left California and
Late one night I let the sound of Pacific surf

Roll through me as I wandered a huge living room
In Santa Monica. My friend Sam Francis spoke:

"The call of the wild, frightening, desolate beauty
That you saw in the outer world—wasn't it
A miasma risen from the depths of your own inner being,
Fragrant and terrifying?
Didn't you come to these waste lands to see
Your own transcendent self?"

It was his serious face
That spoke, he had returned
To his inner face.
The living room reverberated
With deep, heavenly echoes.

Boulder National Park, the Grand Canyon
Dominate all of Arizona, Utah.
There one sees the remains of innumerable rocks
That have sculpted time. Fleets of great ships.
Prisons, monuments, courthouses. Throngs of
Sphinxes, tigers, dinosaurs, whales, phalluses.

　　/ skeletons rub their cheeks
　　together　　　together curse
　　love and death

And Death Valley is not far.
Everything burns in its shimmering haze.
A brief nap in mid-air at the extreme of thirst.
All strength spent, lost in the valleys,
I undo my bones and return to the earth,
Forgetting who I am.
I revert to the elements that form me and
Whisper to myself, "What are you?"

　　/ my face too must be
　　somewhere among these rocks
　　but we will never meet

　　　/ did the prince and princess

who travelled the moon's deserts
admire such landscapes before they died?

In the vocabulary of the North American Indians
(I learned from a book read in the skies above the Rockies),
"To surmise"
"To believe"
"To be uncertain"
"To predict"—the whole kit and caboodle
of shading in white folks' style—
doesn't exist.

You "know" something or you
"Don't know." That's all there is.
There's no "forgiveness,"
And no "sin."
And no "fretting,"
And no "have to," no "intend."

There's no expression that means "we."
They don't say "you and me" either.
"Me and you"—that's all there is.

There's no such thing as "green grass" either.
"Fiber grass"
"Soap foam grass"
"Smoke leaves"—that's all there is.

Then I remembered: in that country
Where the lower leaves are so thick
You can't see an inch ahead,
There, too, was a time when instead of saying
"a pale red flower" they'd point to
Pinks, cherry blossoms, hollyhock,
Peonies, peach blossoms, mimosa, or prince's feather.
There were no "pale blue flowers" either.
There were irises, morning glories, hydrangeas, gentians.

Standing on a craggy cliff,
Some "fiber grass" with flowers exactly like
Japanese valerian whispered:

"Don't dwell on insignificant things.
What you can see is endless,
With your two eyes,
With your one body.
Don't indulge in speculation.
Within you is the infinite."

from *In Sōfu*

(1984)

草府にて

The Principles of Poetry
Shi no Genri

Light and Shadow are not ideas
They are principles

All young creators over the centuries
have been ascetics, the best of their kind
And also worshippers of fornication
smeared with sparkling honey

Yin and Yang are not ideas
They are principles which guide you
to the towering nimbus clouds

Two Eyes
Sōbō

Like birds in flight to the clouds,
coupling and uncoupling
on the path through the sky

The He Called Me
Watakushi to iu Tanin

What a fool this man is
A blessed inlet already shimmering before his eyes

he still goes on lighting the incense of lyric words
trying to pray down another reed plain from heaven

Life Story
Raifu Stoori

The cry of a single bird fills up
                                    : the universe
The silence of two birds overflows

To Art Museums
Bijutsukan e

The first time
I visited an art museum
I remember
how I held my breath
and stole from room to room

Paintings stood
shoulder to shoulder
covered the walls
Some fixed their gazes on me
made me shiver
made me drunk

That sign of scrutiny
from another world
filled the gap
between the painting and me
with the speed of light
In a twinkling
I flew a thousand leagues
a walker in trance

Then I realized:
To see is
to be seen

The first time
I visited an art museum

Snow Outside
Soto wa Yuki

Hammer and chisel make
the most bodily shape of formless things

Words and breath make
the first birth shape of formless things

Valley Stream Reflects the Mountain Light
Keisei no Sanshoku

Between transparency and translucence lies a single line
To which does it belong?

Winter's cudgel slides through
the warm womb of spring

Is not true transparency
true translucence?

Winter's cudgel sliding through the warm womb of spring
is already spring's cudgel   cudgel's spring

Children's Song
Warabeuta

"Going is easy,
returning is hard,
but go if you must"

Still can't forget how
that children's song frightened me,

because as I sang
I knew in my heart

"returning" could
never really

ever be.

On Human Life
Jinsei Ron

A poem can never be finished,
if you ask me.

Isn't it only when you reach for the stars,
only then, that comfort and laughter come?

Nothing wrong with success, of course. What's bad is the brine of it—
The more you drink, the more you thirst, with success.

Before it changes to blood,
the bastard scratches up your throat something awful.

There's no dead end for a corpse, no just so much
and nevermore, if you ask me.

from *What Is Poetry?*

(1985)

詩とはなにか

What Is Poetry? #1
Shi to wa Nani ka 1

It's forever coming at me head on
from the opposite direction
but mostly I just step out of its path
and keep straight on

What Is Poetry? #2
Shi to wa Nani ka 2

It is not
child's play
but   the poet
is a child

What Is Poetry? #3
Shi to wa Nani ka 3

Precisely the process
by which all psychological scenes
proceed to total extinction

Basho

What Is Poetry? #4
Shi to wa Nani ka 4

It doesn't study time
   it ignores the colors of the sky
     like a new born
frog
   it leaps into time-space
     the old pond

What Is Poetry? #6
Shi to wa Nani ka 6

Little things
reflected big   eyes

Big things
come out small   lips

What Is Poetry? #8
Shi to wa Nani ka 8

In the hollow of a hand that polishes
blades of grass, a faint light

in pure darkness

What Is Poetry? #10
Shi to wa Nani ka 10

The kitten
sits on a
plate

How deep is the fur
of those who live
naked

What Is Poetry? #12
Shi to wa Nani ka 12

> To train a word
> you must praise it

> Even if praised to the skies
> a word almost never sings

> Hug the word tightly
> stroke it softly

> Until it releases two sighs
> and long, trailing vowels

What Is Poetry? #15: The Case of a Star

Shi to wa Nani ka 15—Hoshi no Baai

Heaven and earth are being created
  One with the wind
    a star's light
    is rubbing the root of a rock
    that's grown crystals
heating itself alone

What Is Poetry? #17: The Case of Rain
Shi to wa Nani ka 17— Ame no Baai

The rain—
　　drop on the leaf's tip
　　　　firmly
　　pulls together
　in the shape of a drop and then
　　　　　as though sucked forth
　　　　　　　　lengthens out
　　　　all its weight
　　　　concentrated at
　　　　the trembling
　　　　　　tip
　　　　　it falls
　in the shape of firm decision
　s
　t
　r
　a
　i
　g
　h
　t

　d
　o
　w
　n

What Is Poetry? #21
Shi to wa Nani ka 21

Look at that pregnant puss
sinuously

shamelessly
fully content
rubbing her belly on bamboo grass
eyes narrowed in ecstasy

The essence of life
conservatism's pulsating breath

is rubbing her belly on bamboo grass
eyes narrowed
in ecstasy

Ah this!
A wordless song

Shut up behind her eyelids,
penetrating sight

Carried behind in the temperate zone between her legs,
the pink, bad place, softly closed

What Is Poetry? #24: Rules for Its Creation and Interpretation
Shi to wa Nani ka 24—Shi no Seisaku Kaidoku Kokoroe

Dreams[1]:
Involuntary motions of the heart:
you don't even know what you dreamed
until you wake up

When we paint   or   write
we never perceive the totality
of our creating   The totality
resides in the future and the unknown
which is to say in dreams

An obscure marker   is all we can see
The marker itself
takes on indeterminate shape[2]
moment by moment
as the task of creation marches on
In one poem
is an irrepressible dream of flying
That
is the ache at the core of the pistil after fertilization

In one poem
is a dream of a butterfly's escape   to the blue empyrean
That   is the wish   to drown in scarlet flames
engulfing the body[3]

[1]   To write a poem
       to draw a picture
       to fire clay—
       awakening   meditation

[2]   The relation of the marker and creative activity
       may be compared to the conflict between
       technique and air pressure
       in trying to unite the head and tail
       of an aerial oil pipe line

[3] It was a whirlpool who first called
     the straight line a straight line
     It was a full circle who first murmured
     "My own sweet arc!" to the half-circle

Comrades, the Earth is Cold
Hōbai yo Chikyū wa Samui

A single persimmon warms the tree

a pendulum
dangling from
a branch
on earth:

Emperor Bokassa

History
Hisutorii

When I peeled off the murdered man's rags
the naked body of a youth shone back
blindingly holy

When I wrung out the tatters he'd left
a thousand years of time
dripped out
and became a huge river

I saw
we had already become frogs
and on the shores far down river
we were all cheering lustily
celebrating the rediscovery of war

Our greatest geniuses
listed their names
as its inventors

18 Lines Written in Anger

Okotte Kaita Jūhachi Gyō

I have never heard of a mapmaker
who walked the whole world on foot
before mapping it
so colleagues,
my fellow makers of poems,
let's relax   and fill in
the whole map of poetry to every corner

no matter
what dangerous crevasses
its ice floes hide
we can't fall in
we can't fall
except on paper
when we fall
into the real darkness
the map of poetry will be
in someone else's
hands

Red Plum
Ume

Once I broke off   accidentally
a branch of plum before the flowers opened

All the lovely colors
rushed towards the buds
exactly like an army
thronging toward the enemy capital

became blood gushing from the break
suddenly hit
my eyes

It was absolutely uncanny
the way it didn't drip down
in drops
t.h.e. c.o.l.o.r. o.f.

l.i.f.e.!

from *In Blackest Night, the Vacuum Cleaner*

of Heaven Is Full Upon Us

(1987)

ぬばたまの夜、天の掃除器せまつてくる

Song of the Nuclear Submarine 'Thresher', Its Sexual Sea Passage and Suicide

Genshiryoku Sensuikan "Onagazame" no Seiteki na Kōkai to Jisatsu no Uta

> *Written after the nuclear-powered attack submarine USS Thresher was lost at sea 10 April, 1963 on a voyage from Portsmouth, New Hampshire. The Naval Court of Inquiry was held from April 11 to June 5 the same year.—Tr.*

The beginning is perfectly ordinary
a sunny Tuesday morning in mid-April
Thresher pulls quietly out of
a naval port near Boston
no families there to wave goodbye

"Good luck, Dad!
You'll be living at the bottom of the sea, right?
Bring some ghosts back for me, okay, Dad?
Ghosts from a ghost ship — lots and lots!
Wrap them up in devilfish skins,
okay, Dad, please?"

"Sure, Charlie.
And you grow an inch
in the next three months, hear?"

The beginning is perfectly ordinary:
the glow of the sea
the glow of children's cheeks
the glow of the cross-shaped conning tower
SSN 593
the glow of Thresher's belly

Hearts hang on a dream of return
but the real return hangs on the machine
and the machine does not bend to dreams

Now
Thresher's going down, down...

At first shallowly
elaborately, it burrows a hole in the sea surface
    which is at once filled in
    and then opens
    which excites Thresher
The sea radiant
the radiance damp
Thresher's wetness
never stops its dance with the sea

Thresher is
the glans of the United States of America
the lighthouse of hell shining
the searchlight of defensive instinct
from continental shelf to deep seas
over the dark, the fearful unknown
    which only the mighty know

Thresher
lonely male, navigates 100,000 kilometers
never touching land
Thousands of intricate ears, he has
varieties of subtle suckers opening within his belly
to analyze—presto!—the structure of sounds
intuit exactly the enemy's configuration

He seeks the enemy but
fears to meet it:
a male in heat
The energy of atomic destruction
fuels a solitary fever
stirs infinite thirst
plunges him heedlessly into
the mysterious skin of the sea

"Sea   o sea
soft womanly body, you open yourself
in the ebony night shut in by mists
emerald seaweed veiling the ocean floor
sway and bend   oh sleep by me

until my knife-edged soul melts away
until my knife-edged soul melts away"

So now....
flickering tongues of the flytrap grass
sway together
all over the Atlantic's ocean bed and yet

Thresher, solitary male
happy as a babe in a cradle
steams ahead, rocked in bliss
atop the flytrap tongues

never again to see
the light of the sun
heading towards the moment of ecstasy

In April of a certain year in the twentieth century, a United States Navy Court of Inquiry investigated the accidental sinking of the nuclear submarine Thresher at a point 320 kilometers off Boston and made public the following testimony of Lieutenant Junior Grade James Watson of the escort ship Skylark:

"A few seconds past 9:17 A.M., I heard a dull thud as of something collapsing. Five minutes before, a wireless message had come from Thresher, 'Taking up anchor, preparing to surface.' Skylark replied by underwater telephone, 'No sign of boats above water in vicinity, okay to surface.' One minute later, Skylark asked Thresher its course, direction and distance from Skylark, but there was no reply. After that, the captain of the Skylark asked by microphone four times "Are you all right?," but there was no reply. Two minutes later, a message finally came from Thresher but it was almost inaudible. Only the two words "Test depth" could be made out. There seemed to be two or three words before that. Then I heard a sound like torpedoed ships made in World War II, a heavy, dull thud.

"If I had to guess what the inaudible words were that came before the words 'test depth,' I think one of them may have been `exceeding.' But the speaker's tone was not at all excited. That seems odd. The thought crosses my mind, only to be dismissed, that Thresher's disappearance may have been intentional."

The sinking and death of all aboard Thresher was confirmed by discovery of fragments of cork from the vessel and yellow and white gloves. The area where it is presumed to have sunk is 2,500 meters deep. If it sank to the ocean floor, the vessel, unable to withstand the water pressure, would have been crushed flat as a pancake. Under these circumstances, the atomic reactor would be the same as a great quantity of radioactive material compressed into a submarine and thrown into the ocean. Even if there is no nuclear explosion at the core of the reactor, its steel walls will gradually disintegrate over a period of twenty or thirty years.

Did you know
you 129 dead men?
How the sea waters darkened, heavier than steel
when you were crushed in Thresher's body,
ocean morgue?

20 years have passed since then

The quack doctors are on land
their patients buried on an ocean shelf
No matter how often you fathom the ocean's depth
you can never measure
the difference in temperature between hope and despair

In our age the instruments of torture
are remote-controlled. Against them
the voices of children echo in vain

"Please, Dad. Bring some back for me, okay?
Ghosts from a sunken ship —
lots and lots!"

Poem for My Children
Shitashii Kora ni Okuru Shi

Autumn strolls on, infinitely slow, too busy
to spare a backward glance at summer, which it banished long ago

So take a look
    at the fruit's core
    the surface of the scattered leaves
There summer's heroic labors
    have ripened to perfection

Crab Talk
Kani no Hanashi

Look at this Echizen crab,
its lifespan
is about fifteen years for the male
about seven for the female
the darker eggs are the best ones
the female's body is small
because she doesn't shed her shell

To kill them
you put them in fresh water
you put them in and after a while they die
but if the water is too cold
they stay alive
after all they come from way down deep in the sea
about 400 to 700 meters down

You only boil the dead ones
if you boil them alive
all the limbs get torn off
because they thrash about in pain

These days   yeh
our catches aren't what they were
the reason, you say?
it's over-harvesting
the old boats were twenty-five tons
the ones nowadays are a thousand
the costs are completely different
we have to over-harvest or we'd never break even
we mop up the bottom of the sea

The old days?   oh, the boats were little then
and they caught a lot, in the old days
like mountains

Back in Tokyo
Tokyo ni Kaetta

Tokyo's home to so many
people with human faces
    Sometimes you see flower petal ears
    and fruity chins, it's true
People with deeply-carved letters at the corners of their eyes
or lines of music running across their eyebrows
    walk about from time to time, too, mixed in
    But in the end Tokyo's a town
    crammed full with human-faced people
That's what a city is after all—
I know, so I'm not
complaining
    But it's tiring, it really is
    this having a human face all the time
    And it's tiring
    to see nothing but human faces too
In a crowded train
one face like a starry sky
or eyes like the ocean
and a secret yearning fills me

Strange Fragment
Hen na Danpen

Once
in an airplane
I suddenly saw
outside the window
something rather different from
Superman or Spacebird:
A thoroughly wrinkled man
his face contorted
like a topographical map of the Himalayas
covered with thin, corrugated ice
He clung tightly to the airplane's side
so as not to be thrown off
screaming voicelessly
let me in

This human spider gone mad from death
as I'd expected
from a little before
was my own self

He and I
traveled face to face for some time until
the wrinkled one was thrown off and disappeared
The experience made
the way I lived—nourished on
airline food, in the illusory safety
of a seat belt—
seem unspeakably coarse

It made my life mortal

Morning Prayer
Asa no Inori

God,

I want thoughts
spun to the clarity of a spider's thread
become radiance itself

But they will surely form a web
capture a beautiful butterfly
and reduce her to a wind-blown corpse

In the Style of Goethe
Gyoete Fū

The world
can put up with anything
except continuing happiness—
that it can not endure
And so God
gave
eternity's shadow,
called beauty—
fleeting surface and also essence—
only to ephemeral things

Autumn Melancholy
Shūshi Hen

Autumn eggs
surround at a distance the heart's bay
tens and hundreds
fully ripened
in rows

If this is an illusion
then what
is the reality

This landscape is complete
even the breeze
filled with wind
is singing

Twin hemispheres
floating in the bay!

You are not a woman's breasts
but neither are you
the blue sky's testicles
Boats harbored in my dream

Inscrutable
twin hemispheres!

Since you won't allow me
even a tentative touch
I have only
my own words to embrace
in the heart's bay....

Twin hemispheres
watched over
by autumn eggs!

Tokyo Dirge
Tokyo Banka

We walk beneath cherry blossoms
They've begun to fall

Everything decays   you, too

In the depths of spring
the corpse of spring

From there the flowers   explode to heaven again

The flower viewers on the highway
race towards hell

As though they mean to make the maple leaves by evening

Songs for the Four Seasons: Summer Song
Shiki no Uta Natsu no Uta

Reptiles:
embodiment of
power and life,
they never
align themselves
to the straight
and narrow

Praise the glory
of this tribe
that comes from the sea
weaves the earth together
and again
returns
to the waves

Autumn Song
Aki no Uta

Night is a big blue chair
Along its back creep
fingers of eyeless, noseless
Chaos,
ready to twirl and twist us
like holy flowers
in the Buddha's hand

Yesterday
from the furthest reaches of the sky
we heard its footsteps,
brightly splashing
in the waves along the shore

Winter Song
Fuyu no Uta

Snail's regressed
to egghood   again

for subterranean nurture
of the spring it's never met

Spring Song
Haru no Uta

Another saffron robe
awakened by the Buddha's words
is already turning at its hem
into a great river

Even though countless deaths
flow down it without pause
the river of Time until its very end
is a flow of words which transcends the human

from *Messages to the Waters of My Hometown*

(1989)

故郷の水へのメッセージ

Thus Spoke the Bird of Passage
Wataridori Kaku Katariki

The humans call my endless flight
in a splendid phrase
"the celestial navigation of birds"

All I do is obey
the deoxyribonucleic acid
cross oceans braving the wind

I ride the stream of pure biogenetic time

Unlike human nations and civilizations
history can't contain me

The Tale of a Star #1
Hoshi Monogatari a

A star is
an infinitely
and slowly
collapsing
being

My favorite star
scrawls graffiti
all over the sky and
never bothers to
read them back

Now there's someone
I can take off my hat to!

The Tale of a Star #2
Hoshi Monogatari b

Stars cluster near far large small
and people paint constellations on them as they please

Child suicides seek a gentle chair in that sky
a chair they never found in life, a chair to sit in at last

Poor things, you've got it wrong! In the great sky above
you'll never find the constellation of ultimate joy

Such Women Where Are You?
Sono yō na Onnatachi yo, doko ni iru no ka

Green Women
Midori no Onna

Midori, our word for green today, was not the name of a color in its original classical meaning. It meant "new bud" or "young branch," as in this poem by Ki no Tsurayuki,

I full my beloved's robe
in spring, and with
each rain that falls
the color of the fields' *midori*
grows brighter still

Midori here means "the new buds on the trees and plants" rather than the color green itself. The rain makes them brighter, just as beating, or fulling, the cloth after washing stretches it back to shape and brings out the color.

All Japanese names for colors were originally the names of things. *Ai,* for example, was first the name for the indigo plant; only later did it come to mean the color itself.

Midorigo means a human bud, a baby. The way a baby wiggles its arms and legs in its sleep is just the way the new buds bob on the branch. A single word expresses the whole idea.

The little girls who waited on courtesans in the Yoshiwara pleasure quarters were often called *midori,* doubtless a reference to "new buds."

But something just as important and interesting is involved here.

The natural world is full of green; it is found everywhere. And yet, as dyers know, it is impossible to extract *midori* dye from any one single thing.

To get dyers' green you must mix blue and yellow. This fact testifies to the profound mystery of the natural world.

Green: the color spread most widely over the Earth.

In its essence, an intermingling of different colored matter. Colors bleeding into one another. *Midori,* the color of life. A hybrid, impure from inception. And therefore, profound.

Such women, where are you?

Blue Women
Ao no Onna

Candy and pastry come in many different colors but blue, I am certain, is the one used least.

Something holds us back from biting into a pastry of midnight blue or devouring a candy blue as the clearest ocean. Flesh intuits the meaning behind the common image of blue as a cold color.

My beloved Kandinsky said "Blue is the most celestial of all colors."

Yellow, a warm color, is, by contrast, the earthiest.

"Blue increases thickness, increases depth, and so invites man to the infinite and awakens in him a longing for the pure and then the transcendent."

And so, blue is almost never used for sweets. They are too delicious, too earthly, too intimately connected with fleshly joy.

Scoop up the ocean, soar through the sky—no matter how far you go, you can't touch their brimming blue. Water's transparent; so is the sky.

Blue: a color without peer, beyond reality. Because it is the color of light. *The Blue Flower, The Bluebird:* the color of longing, of an absent bird.

Such women, where are you?

Photos and Illustrations

Photo: Ishikawa Shūko

Aizawa Kaneko and Ōoka Makoto in Numazu, shortly before their marriage in 1957. Ōoka, who was then a reporter on the foreign desk of the Yomiuri Shimbun, is holding a French newspaper.

Ōoka in the garden of the Jindaiji house with the cat Tom and the dog
Hayato, in the mid-1980s

Ōoka Makoto at his desk in the Mitaka house, mid-1960s.

Ōoka Makoto and Kaneko in New York, March 2000.

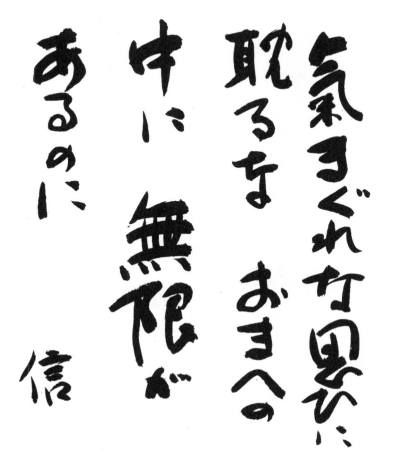

Calligraphy by Ōoka Makoto. From "Kashū Mokkei" (California: Unvoiced Harmonies)

Kimagure na omoi ni
fukeru na   Omae no
naka ni   mugen ga
aru no ni

Don't indulge in
speculation   Within
you   is
the infinite

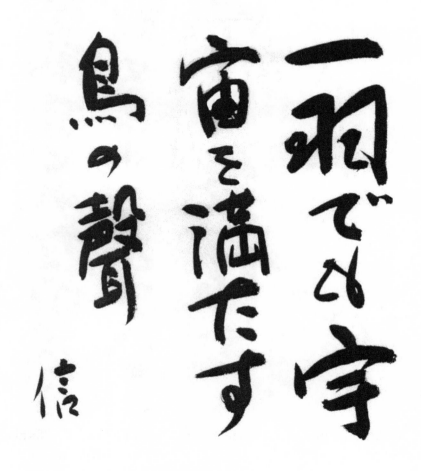

Calligraphy by Ōoka Makoto. From "Raifu Stōrii" (Life Story)

Ichiwa de mo u
chū wo mitasu
tori no koe

The cry of a single bird fills up the universe

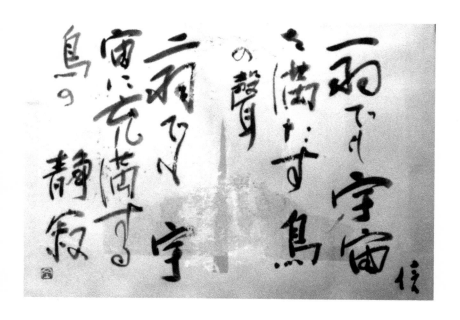

Calligraphy by Ōoka Makoto. From "Raifu Stōrii" (Life Story)

Ichiwa de mo uchū
wo mitasu tori
no koe
Niwa de mo   u
chū ni jūman suru
tori no   seijaku

The cry of a single bird fills up
the universe
The silence of two birds overflows
the universe

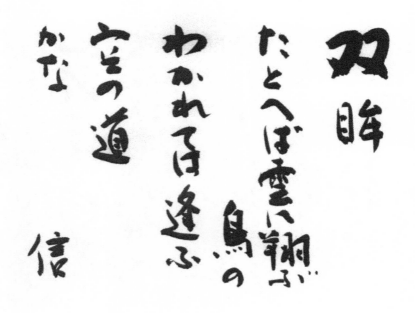

Calligraphy by Ōoka Makoto. "Sōbō" (Two Eyes)

Sōbō
Tatoeba kumo ni tobu
            tori no
wakarete wa au
sora no michi
kana

Two Eyes
Like birds in flight to the clouds,
coupling and uncoupling
on the path through the sky

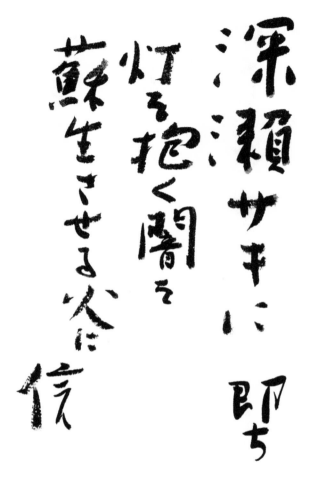

Ōoka gave personally inscribed copies of all his books to his wife. This inscription reads:

"Fukase Saki ni sunawachi
hi wo daku yami wo
sosei saseru hi ni
Makoto"

"To Fukase Saki, the fire that brings the light-embracing darkness back to life—Makoto"

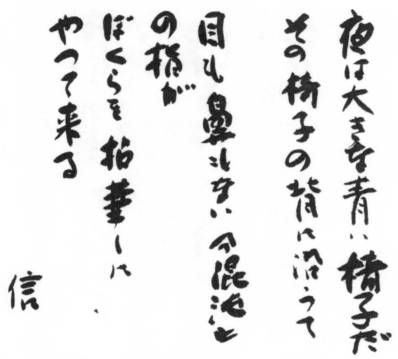

Calligraphy by Ōoka Makoto. From "Aki no Uta" (Autumn Song)

Yoru wa ōki na aoi isu da
Sono isu no se ni soute
me mo hana mo nai konton
no yubi ga
bokura wo nenge shi ni
yatte kuru

Night is a big blue chair
Along its back creep
fingers of eyeless, noseless
Chaos
ready to twirl and twist us
like holy flowers
in the Buddha's hand

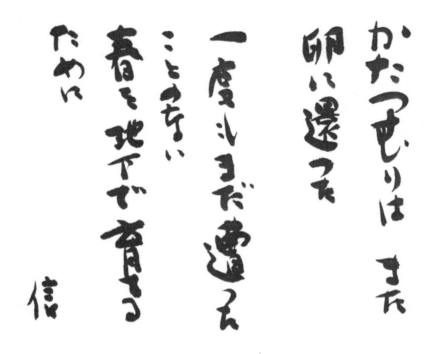

Calligraphy by Ōoka Makoto. From "Fuyu no Uta" (Winter Song)

Katatsumuri wa mata
tamago ni kaetta

ichido mo mada atta
koto no nai
haru wo chika de sodateru
tame ni

Snail's regressed
to egghood   again

for subterranean nurture
of the spring it's never met

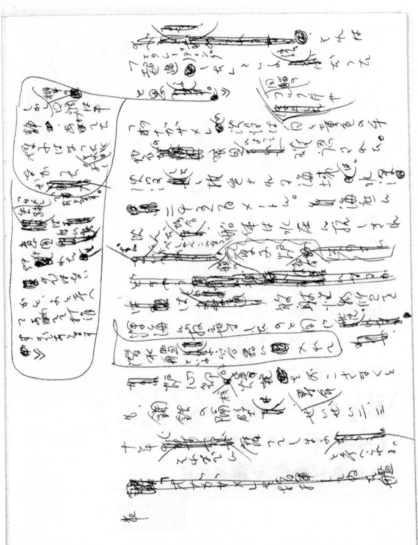

The manuscript for "Denshiryoku Sensuikan 'Onagazame' no Seiteki na Kōkai to Jisatsu no Uta" (Song of the Nuclear Submarine Thresher, Its Sexual Sea Passage and Suicide), from one of his many notebooks. Very few of his poems show such evidence of heavy revision. This is from the prose section of the poem, which is a partial translation of the testimony given at the hearings to determine the cause of the disaster.

Another page from Ōoka's notebooks, this one containing part of "Kaze no Setsu" (All About the Wind). Typical of the notebook, it shows only a few marks of revision. The many revisions in "Song for the Nuclear Submarine Thresher" suggest that Ōoka was exploring new territory.

合ひが、そこにはある。

わが敬愛するカンディンスキーは定義する、「青は典型的に天上の色」。対するに暖色の「黄」は典型的に地上の色。

「濃さを増し深みを増せば、青はそれだけ人を無限の世界へ誘い、かれのうちに、純枠なものへのあこがれ、最後には超感覚のものへのあこがれを、よび醒ますようになる。*」

菓子といふ地上的な、肉の歓喜に直結した美味なるものに使はれることが少ないのは、理由なきことではない。海の水をいくらすくつてみても、空高くいかに舞い上がつてみても、深々とたたへてゐた青の色はどこにもない。水は透明、空も透明。

青の色はまことに現実の彼方の色。それは光の色だからだ。「青い花」、「青い鳥」。憧れの色、ゐない鳥。

そのやうな女たちよ、どこにゐるのか。

* 『芸術における精神的なものについて』（西田秀穂訳による）

原文の終わり

そのやうな女たちよ、どこにゐるのか

一 緑の女

ミドリといふ語は、古語本来の意味においては、色の名でなかったといふ。それは新芽や若枝をいふことばだつた。

わがせこが衣はる雨ふるごとに野べの緑ぞいろまさ
りける　　　　　　　　　　　　　　　　つらゆき

ここに萌えでた「緑」も、色より先に「草木の新芽」そのものだつた。

日本の色名一般がモノそのものの呼び名だつた。「藍色」といへば藍といふ草の名がそのまま色になったのだ。

ミドリゴは、人間の新芽のことだ。赤ん坊が寝たまま手足をうち振る姿は、新芽のさかんな活動そのもの。言葉はまことに多くを語る。

吉原の禿の名に、ミドリが愛用されたのも、「新芽」なればまことに納得。

しかしここにもう一つ、重要にして興味ぶかい事象がある。

染色家たちは、自然界いたる所にこれほど溢れてゐる緑色が、単一の「緑」といふ染料としては、決してそのまま取り出せないと知つてゐる。

緑色を染料として得るためには、青と黄を混ぜ合せねばならないのだ。自然界の神秘を語る意味深長な事実である。

地球を最も広範に覆ふ色は緑。

その実体は、異質な色の物質の掛け合はせ。染まり合ひ。

「緑」といふ生命の色は、はじめから純一ではない混ざりもの。だから深い。

そのやうな女たちよ、どこにゐるのか。

二 青の女

和菓子にせよ洋菓子にせよ、菓子にさまざま色彩があ
る中で、最も使用頻度の低い色は青ではないのか。

澄みきつた青海原色、また紺碧の菓子を出されて、いきなりむしやむしや食べるのは、何となく畏れ多きに似た感じだ。寒色と呼ばれる青の、肉体に直観される意味

*Translation on
pages 91–92*

星ものがたり　a

星は無限にゆるやかに
崩壊してゐる生きものだ
おれの好きなあの星は
自分が夜空に書いたものを
一度も読んだりすることはない
なんといふ素敵なやつだらう

星ものがたり　b

遠近大小とりまぜた星の群れに
人間は勝手に星座を思ひ描く
はじめて坐れる優しい椅子をあの空に求める
自殺する子どもは子どもで
どつちにしたつて存在してはをらんのだ
幸福の究極の星座なんて　空の上には

詩集《故郷の水へのメッセージ》から

渡り鳥　かく語りき

人間どもはおれの限りない飛翔を
鳥の天体航法と呼んでくれる
うまいことをいふものだ

おれはただ
デオキシリボ核酸の命ずるままに
海を渡る　荒天を衝いて

おれが属してゐるのは
生物の純粋な遺伝時間の泉だ

人間の国家とか文明のやうに
歴史に属したりはしてゐない

Translation on
pages 85–88

四季のうた

　一　夏のうた
爬虫類こそ力づよい生命の形
一瞬たりとも直線に同調しない
讃へよ　海から来て地を縫ひ合はせ
再び波に帰つてゆく栄えある種族を

　二　秋のうた
夜は大きな青い椅子だ
その椅子の背に沿うて
目も鼻もない《混沌》の指が
ぼくらを拈華しにやつてくる
波打際のピチャリピチャリの足音が
空のはてから昨日明かるく聞こえてゐた

　三　冬のうた
かたつむりは　また
卵に還つた
一度もまだ遭つたことのない
春を地下で育てるために

　四　春のうた
また一枚　仏陀のコトバに愕いた
黄色い衣が
裾の方で
大河に変らうとしてゐる
生類の死が
どんどん上から流れてきても
時の河は末の未まで
人を超えたコトバの流れでできてゐる

Translation on
page 84

東京挽歌

散りそめた桜の下を
ぼくらは歩く

みな腐るのだ　あなたも

春の奥には
春のむくろ

そこから花は　また天に噴き

高速道路の花見客は
地獄へのんのん走つてゐる

夕紅葉まで到りつくがに

Translation on
page 83

秋思篇

秋の卵は
心の湾を遠巻きにして
何十となく
むつちり実つて
列なつてゐる

これらが仮象
であるとしたら
どこに実体があるといふ

これは充実した風景だ
微風さへ
風を孕んで
歌つてゐる

その湾に浮かぶ
双半球よ

女の胸乳ではない
だが天の青い
陰嚢でもない
ぼくの夢の泊り船

不可知の
双半球よ

いちどもぼくに
さはることを許さないので
今ではぼくの
ことばとだけ
抱き合つてゐる
心の湾の……

秋の卵に見守られてゐる
双半球よ

朝の祈り

神よ わたしは——

蜘蛛の糸の澄んだ形に還元されて
輝きそのものとなるやうな
思想を持ちたい

だがそれは　必ずや巣の構造を持ち
美しい蝶を捕らへて
風に揺れるむくろに彼女を還元するだらう

ギョエテ風

世の中のものは
どんなものでも我慢できる
だが幸福な日の連続だけは
我慢できない
だから神は
移ろひやすいものにだけ
美といふ世にも移ろひやすい
衣裳にして本質なる
永遠の影
を与へたのだ。

Translation on
page 80

へんな断片

あるときぼくは
飛行機で
ふと窓の外に
スーパーマンとも
宇宙鳥ともおよそ違つた
顔中ゆがんで
皺くちやな
細氷に蔽はれてゐる
ヒマラヤの地形図様の
しわしわ男が
ぴつたり機体に張りついて
振り落とされまい
中へ入れろと
声なく叫んでゐるのを見た

この死にもの狂ひの人蜘蛛は
さつきから

予期した通り
このぼくだつた

こいつが遂に
振り落とされて消え去るまで
皺くちや男と顔見合はせて
ずつと旅する経験は
機内食で養はれつつ
座席ベルトで安全を
幻想してゐる生き方を
むしやうに卑しいものに思はせ

わが人生を
儚くさせた

東京に帰つた

東京には
ニンゲンの顔したヒトがいつぱいゐる
花びらの耳
木の実の顎もときどきある
目尻に深く文字の皺を彫つてるヒト
眉毛に楽曲の線引いてるヒトも
時には混じつて歩いてをる
でも東京は　とにかく
ニンゲンの顔したヒトの溢れてるまちだ
都会つてものは
さういふもんだと思ふから
それでいいのだ
しかしいつもニンゲンの顔をしつづけるのは
くたびれることだ
ニンゲンの顔ばかり見て過ごすのも
くたびれることだ
顔が星空をしてゐる人

目が大洋をしてゐる人が
満員電車に一人でもゐると
そつと憧れてしまふ

Translation on
page 78

別の日　越前で蟹を見た

ごらんのこの
越前蟹の年齢ですが
雄は十五年くらるです
雌は七年くらるです
卵は黒つぽいのが上等です
雌の体が小さいのは
雌は脱皮しませんから

死なせるには
真水につけます
つけておくとゆつくり死にます
ただし水が冷たすぎると
なかなか死なんです
なにしろ四〇〇メートルから七〇〇ぐらるの
深海に棲んどるですから
死んだのを茹でるのです

生きたまま茹でましたら
手足がぜんぶもげてしまひます
苦しがつて暴れますゆゑ

近ごろは　ええ
水揚げは減つてます
理由ですか
乱獲です
昔の船は二五トン
今の船は一〇〇〇トン
コストがぜんぜん違ひます
乱獲しなくちやならないのです
海の底までさらひます
昔ですか　小さな船でねえ
昔はそれはよく獲れました
山のやうに

Translation on
pages 76-77

百二十九人の死者たち
きみらは知つてゐたか
水は鋼鉄よりも暗くて重いと
「ヲナガザメ」の胎内で
押しひしやげられた深海のモルグ……

あれから二十年余りが過ぎた

希望と絶望の温度差は測れなかつた
水深はいかに測れても
患者は大洋の棚の上
やぶ医者どもは地上にゐて

遠隔操縦されてゐる
われらの時代の拷問装置に
子どもらの声がむなしく響く

オネガヒダヨ　トツテキテネ
ユウレイセンノ　ユウレイ
タクサン

親しい子らに贈る詩

秋は無限の緩やかさで歩むことに忙がしく
とうに追放した夏をば振返らない

だからごらん　果実の芯　散る木の葉の表面にも
夏の偉大な仕事は　ありありと成就される

「ナガザメ」は無電で「上ゲカヂとつて浮上の用意」と伝へてきた。「ヒバリ」は水中電話によつて「付近海上船影なし、浮上オーケイ」と答へた。一分後、「ヒバリ」は「サメ」に進路・方向、本艦との距離を問うたが、応答がなかつた。その後四回、「ヒバリ」艦長はマイクロフォンで、「大丈夫か」と呼びかけたが、応答はなかつた。さらに二分たつて、やつと「サメ」から連絡がきたが、聴取きはめて困難、わづかに「試験深度」の二語を聞きとれたのみ。その二語の前に二、三の単語があつたやうだ。つづいて耳は、かつて第二次大戦中に、船が魚雷で吹つとばされたあのときの震動と同じ響きを感じた。重苦しい、ドスンといふ音がした。

「試験深度」といふ二語の前の、明瞭には聞きとれなかつた単語について、もしあへて言へと命令されるなら、それはたぶん、「乗越えて」といふ語だつたと思ふ。「サメ」失跡は意図的に実行されたものではないかと、ふと想像して、あわてて打消すのであります》

「ヲナガザメ」の沈没と全員死亡は、同艦のコルク片や白と黄色の手袋類の発見によつて確認された。沈没したと推定される海域は、水深三千五百メートル。海底に沈んだ場合、船体は水圧に抗しきれず、ペシヤンコになる。艦の原子炉部分は、あたかも大量の放射性物質を、潜水艦といふ容器に入れて深海に投棄したのと同じ状況になるわけだが、たとへ炉心部に核爆発が起きなかつたとしても、その鋼鉄の隔壁は、寿命せいぜい二、三十年、徐々に腐つてしまふだらう。

おれの利ごころ失せるまで

ああ　かくて
虫とり草のチロチロ揺れる舌が
大西洋の全海底で
いつせいにそよいでゐるのに
孤独な牡の「ヲナガザメ」は
揺りかごの赤ん坊の快さで
うつとりと揺すられて進む
虫とり草の舌の上へ

ふたたびは
太陽光を見ることのない
恍惚の瞬間めざして

一九××年四月、ボストン沖合三百二十数キロ地点で沈没した原子力潜水艦「ヲナガザメ」
の遭難について調査中の米海軍査問委員会は、護衛艦「ヒバリ」号の航海士ワトソン中尉の
次のやうな証言を明らかにした。
《午前九時十七分数秒すぎ、押しつぶしたやうななにぶい音響が聞こえた。その五分前、「ヲ

海の穴はたちまちふさがり
また開き
「ヲナガザメ」を興奮させる
海は光り
光は濡れ
「ヲナガザメ」は濡れて
海と接触をくりかへす

かれこそは
合衆国の性の亀頭
大陸棚から深海へむけて
強者だけが知る未知の恐怖の暗闇を
防禦本能の探照灯で照らしつつゆく
地獄の灯台

「ヲナガザメ」は
陸地に接することもなく
十万キロを航行する孤独な牡だ
かれは持つ　数千の精巧な耳を

胴体にひらく敏感な吸盤の類は
雑音の形態をたちどころに分析し
敵の形態に鋭敏に吸ひつく

かれは敵を求めつつ
敵との出会ひに恐怖する
発情期の牡だ
原子破壊のエネルギーが
かれの孤独な興奮を持続させ
限りない渇きをかきたて
海の神秘な膚の奥へ
しゃにむに突き進ませる

海よ　おお海
身をひらくやはらかい牝のからだよ
水底に生ふる玉藻よ
ぬばたまの夜霧ごもりに
うちなびき　寄り寝してくれ
おれの利ごころ失せるまで

Translation on
pages 73-76

詩集《ぬばたまの夜、天の掃除器せまつてくる》から

原子力潜水艦「ヲナガザメ」の性的な航海と自殺の唄

はじめは何の変哲もない
晴れわたつた四月なかばの火曜の朝だ
ボストンに近い海軍基地を
見送る家族の一人もなしに
静かに離れて旅に出る

「グッド・ラック　パパ
海ノソコデクラシテクルノネ
オネガヒダヨ　トツテキテネ
ユウレイセンノ　ユウレイ　タクサン
チヤウチンアンカウノ　フクロニクルンデ
イイカイ　パパ」

「オーケイ　チャーリー
三月(みつき)たつたら　一インチ
伸びてるんだぞ」

はじめは何の変哲もない
海の輝き
ちびどもの頬の輝き
十字架形の司令塔の輝き
SS(N)593
「ヲナガザメ」の胴の輝き

希望は帰投に
帰投は機構にかかつてゐるが
機構は希望に関与しない
いまはただ
「ヲナガザメ」は沈むのみ

手はじめに浅く
たんねんに海面を掘る

*Translation on
page 71*

梅

誤つて　花開く前の
紅梅の枝を折つてしまつたことがある

都めがけて殺到する
軍勢さながら
つぼみにむかつて奔流する
色素どもは

折れ口の鮮血となつて
ぼくの目を
ハッシと打つた

タラタラとしたたらないのが
あれほどぷきみな
ことはなかつた
イノチの

イロ！

あかときを
冬鳥むれて
湧くごとし
こはわが庭で
信じがたしも

訳註：大岡信の確認の上（1995年）英訳で最後の5行を省いた。

Translation on
pages 69–70

ヒストリー

殺された男のボロを剝ぐと
眩ゆいばかり神々しい
青年の裸身だつた

彼が遺したボロをしぼると
千年の歳月が
したたり
したたり
溢れて大河となつた

見ればもう
ぼくらは蛙になつて
遙か下流のザラ瀬で
いやしい歓呼の声をあげつつ
戦争といふものを再発見してゐた

ぼくらのうち最大の天才たちが
それの発明者に
名を列ねてゐるのだ

怒つて書いた十八行

地図の作者が
みづから世界のすみずみまで
踏破してみて地図をかいたといふ話は
聞いたことがない

だからご同輩
詩の作者らよ
安んじて　われらも
すみずみまで詩の地図を
自信をもつて埋めませう

氷島に
どんな危険なクレヴァスが
あつたとしても
われらはけつして落ちはしない
落ちるのはいつも
紙の上

ほんとに闇に落ちるときは
詩の地図は
別のだれかの手の中にある

Translation on
pages 67–68

朋輩よ地球はさむい

木まもりの柿一個。

ブラリン
プラン
地球の枝に
揺れてゐる。

ボカサ皇帝。

（註3）
直線は渦巻きによつて
はじめて「直線よ」と呼ばれ
半円の弧は全円によつて
はじめて「わが弧よ」と囁かれる

詩とはなにか　24──詩の制作＝解読　こころえ

夢は（註1）
醒めてみないと
見てゐたことさへわからない
こころの不随意筋の運動

ぼくらはゑがき　また　書くとき
自分が象りつつあるものの
全容を認識しない　全容は
未来と未知に　すなはち夢に属す

見えるのはただ　漠たる目標
して目標はそれ自体
象る作業の進展につれ
刻々と不定形に変容する（註2）

ひとつの詩には
抑へがたい飛翔の夢がある

それは
受胎後の雌蕊の　中心へ向かふ疼きそのもの

ひとつの詩には
群青の天へ逃亡する　蝶の夢がある

それは
わが身を焼き滅ぼす紅蓮体への　投身願望そのもの（註3）

（註1）
詩を作ること
絵を描くこと
土を焼くこと──
醒めて行ふ メディテーション

（註2）
目標と制作行為の関係は
空中給油のオイル管が
首尾よく接合されるまでの
風圧と技術の争ひに類推されよう

Translation on
page 65

詩とはなにか

21

見よ　かの孕み猫を
しなやかに
臆面もなく
満ち足りて

目を細めてゐる
笹に腹をこすつて

命の本質
ぴくぴく息づく保守性が
目を細めてゐる
いま笹に腹をこすつて

ああこの！
ことばなきうたよ

瞼の裏には蔵つてゐるナ
炯々たる眼光を

後ろ肢の温帯には下げてゐるナ
ふうわり閉ざせるピンクの悪所を

Translation on
pages 63–64

詩とはなにか　15——星のばあい

天地が創造されつつある——
風と区別のつかない
星の光は
水晶を生やした岩の
根もとをこすつて
ひとり熱くなつてゐる

詩とはなにか　17——雨のばあい

雨は
　葉さきのしづくのなかで
　　しつかり
しづくのかたちに
　ちぢこまつてから
吸はれるやうに
　引き出される

ぷるぷる震へる
　　尖端に
　　　重みをすべて
　　　　集中して
墜ちてゆく
　　思ひ決したすがたで
まつすぐ

Translation on
pages 61–62

詩とはなにか　10

猫の仔が
皿のうへに乗つてゐる

素ッ裸で生きるものは
なんと毛深き

詩とはなにか　12

ことばを鍛へるには
ことばを誉めねばならぬ

誉めそやしても
ことばが歌ひだすのは稀れだ

しづかに撫でてやれ
ことばの胸をぐつと摑んで

母音がながあく尾を引いて
溜息を二つ洩らすまで

Translation on
pages 59–60

詩とはなにか 6

小さなことを
大きく映す　眼

大きなことを
小さく発する　唇

詩とはなにか 8

とがった草を磨く
てのひらに薄明り
まだ真暗だ

Translation on pages 57–58

詩とはなにか　3

すべての心理てき風景の
ぜつめつしてゆく
過程そのもの

詩とはなにか　4

時の意味を学ばず
空の彩りを見ず
たつたいまうまれたばかりの
蛙として
時空に跳ねる
古池

*Translation on
pages 55-56*

詩集《詩とはなにか》から

詩とはなにか　1

むかうからたえず
ぶつかつてくるが
わたしはいくらでも
よけてとほつてゐるもの

詩とはなにか　2

こどものあそび
ではない
だが　しじんは
こどもです

*Translation on
pages 52–53*

わらべうた

「往き」はよろしい、
「還り」は怖い、通りやんせ。

わらべの唄の
今に忘れぬ怖さとは、

唄ひながら
ひそかに知つてゐたからだ、

「還り」なんて
ほんとは決して
ありはせぬこと。

人生論

おれは思はない、一篇の詩に
完成がありうるとは。

ただ達しえぬものに挑む、そのときだけ
人はたしかに持てると思ふ、ゆとりと笑ひを。

成功も悪くはない。悪いのはただ、
飲めば飲むほど渇きを産む塩水なのだ、成功は。

血液に成り変る前に
こいつは咽喉をばりばりに荒してしまふ。

おれは思はない、一個の死体に
過不足なく完成された終りがあるとは。

Translation on pages 50–51

外は雪

槌と鑿でつくるのは
かたちなきもののきはみのかたち

言葉と息でつくるのは
かたちなきもののはじまりのかたち

谿声の山色

真の透明と半透明の境界は
透明か　半透明か

冬の棍棒がさし貫いてゐる
春の胎蔵界を

真の半透明ではないのか
真の透明とは

春の胎蔵界をさし貫く冬の棍棒は
すでに春の棍棒　棍棒の春だ

Translation on
page 49

美術館へ

生まれてはじめて
美術館に入つた日のこと
おぼえてゐるのは
いつのまにか息をひそめて
廊から廊を伝つてゐたこと

肩を竝べて壁に立つ
たくさんの絵のなかに
ときどきじつと
ぼくを見つめてゐるものがゐた
それがぼくを慄へさせ
ぼくを酔はせた

彼方からの
凝視の気配が
眼前の絵からぼくまでの距離を
言ひやうのない遙けさで満たし

ぼくはそこでは
一瞬に千里を飛ぶ
夢うつつの
歩行者だつた

見ることは
見られることと
そのとき知つた

生まれてはじめて
美術館に入つた日のこと

Translation on
pages 47–48

私といふ他人

この男はなんといふ愚か者だらう
祝福された入江はすでに目の前に揺れてゐるのに
せつせと抒情的な言葉の護摩を焚いて
別の葦原を天から祈りおろさうといふのだ

ライフ・ストーリー

一羽でも宇宙を満たす鳥の声
二羽でも宇宙に充満する鳥の静寂

Translation on
pages 45–46

詩集《草府にて》から

詩の原理

「光」と「影」は概念ではない。
原理だ。

諸世紀の創造する若者はすべて、
とびきりの禁欲家だつた。そして、

きらきら輝く蜜にまみれた
姦淫の、崇拝者だつた。

「陰」と「陽」は概念ではない。
積乱雲をみちびく原理だ。

双眸

たとへば雲に翔ぶ鳥の
わかれては逢ふ
空の道
かな

岩場に立つて
女郎花そつくりの花をつける
「筋の草」はささやいた、

よしないことを詮索するな、
見るべきものは限りなく、
おまへの眼は二つ。
からだは一つ。
気まぐれな思ひに耽るな、
おまへの中に無限があるのに。

「われ」といふ言ひ方も
「汝と我」といふ語順もない。
「我と汝」、ただそれだけだ。

「緑の草」と言ふこともない。
「筋の草」
「石鹸泡の草」
「煙の葉」、それだけだ。

僕はその時憶つてゐた、
下葉茂れる
一寸さきも見えないほどの森の国にも
「淡紅の花」といふかはり
撫子、桜、桃、葵、牡丹、合歓ノ木、蓼と指示した
ころもあつたと。
「薄青の花」もなかつた。
桔梗、朝顔、紫陽、竜胆、それらはあつた。

〜 骸骨が頬寄せ合つて
死のことや愛のことなど
呪ひあふらし

「死の谷」も遠くはない。
あそこではすべてが燃えるかげろふ。
渇きのはての束の間の宙づりの眠り。
力尽き、谷間を迷ひ
骨をほどいて地に還るとき
人は忘れる、自分が「だれ」であるかを。
人は自分を形づくる物質の素性（そせい）に戻り
「おまへは何?」とおのれにささやく。

〜 わが顔も居ならぶ岩のいづくにか
あらむされども
相逢はざらん

〜 月の砂漠をゆきし王子とお姫さま

こんな景色を愛（め）で
果つらむか

北米インディアンの語彙の中には
（ロッキー山脈上空で読んだ本が
ぽくに教へた）
「と推測する」
「と信じる」
「かどうか疑はしい」
「と予測する」
それらすべての白人式ぼかし語のむれは
存在しない。

きみは何かを「知つてゐる」
さなくば「知らぬ」。それだけだ。
「赦し」もない。
「罪」もない。
「くよくよ」もない。
「ねばならぬ」も「つもりだ」もない。

見るべきものの多様さに
ただ従へ。
ただ圧し倒されよ。
さて圧し倒せ。
よしないことは詮索するな。
ただ過ぎよ。
過ぎゆきつつ、
とどまるものに挨拶せよ。
挨拶せよ、とどまるものに。

さう僕に語つたのは、
幹白いアスペン林の柱廊のはてに鎮もる
フィッシュレイクの蒼白い波風だつたが
旅のはて、十月なかば
熱波の去つたカリフォルニアの
太平洋の波音に身を染ませつつ
サンタモニカの広い居間をさまよふ夜ふけ
僕の友フランシスはかう言つたのだ、

「おまへが外部世界に見た
荒々しく、怖るべき
荒寥の美のよびかけは、
より深く、おまへ自身の内面から
立ちのぼつてきた、かぐはしくも恐ろしい
瘴気ではなかつたのか。
おまへはおまへを超えたおまへへ
見るために、荒地へやってきたのではないか」

さう言つた人は
まじめな顔に還つてゐた、彼の内なる顔に。
そのとき居間は
深い天の反響のうちにあつた。

アリゾナ、ユタに蟠踞する
岩石公園、大峡谷に
人は見た、無数の岩が時を刻んだ残りかす
巨船、牢獄、大建築、裁判所のむれ。
スフィンクス、虎、恐龍、鯨、陽根のむれ。

Translation on
pages 39–43

調布 Ⅷ

　　某婦人に呈す

否定できない　どうしても。

とるに足らない秘密だと思ふのだが

詩の秘密がある。

ただそれだけのことの中に

いい詩を読めば心はよろこぶ。

どんな嫌ひな人間が書いた詩でも

加州黙契

カワカワと鳴る朴の枯葉

ばらばらと散る夜ふけの紅葉

下葉茂れる

一寸さきも見えないほどの日本の森を

天ざかる向う岸に置いて忘れ

黄金の葉なすアスペンの森林をゆく。

ヘアスペンは黄に照り映えて

キャニオンの赤岩の背に

秋たちにけり

ヘアスペンはいてふに似たれ

葉は硬し

カラカラ鳴ればこころおどろく

むなしいことを詮索するな。

気まぐれな思ひに耽るな。

Translation on
pages 37–38

「ああ。　もう。　早くぶち壊さう。

らくらくと息をしよう、　らくらくと」

だれもが待つてゐるその声は、

ひとりひとりの中にあつた。

そのひとことを発するのが、

なにしろ一番恐ろしい

ことなのだつた。

韻府

泉に告ぐ。

なんぢ、

詩なれば、

洩らすなよ。

Translation on
pages 36–37

ならんで立つぼくらの横に、
べつのぼくらが
ふかぶかと眠つてゐるのが。
おお 苦しみも知らず
眠つてゐるのが。

だからぼくは何度でも
雪の焔に身を運ばせる。
海くぐり抜け、
月のきみを
空高く浮かべてやるのだ、
昔の沼津の夕陽の彼方へ。

脳府

あしたはあしたの風 ですか

恐ろしいことがきつと起こる。
どの家のどの部屋もさう感じてゐた。
そろりそろり堡塁を築きにかかつたひともゐた。
逃げこむつもりの下水溝で、もう溺れちやつたひともゐた。

まちの第一細胞室から、第百四十億室まで、
わづかな風圧変化にも、ショックと緊張。

それでも楽の音(ね)はひびき、恋もあつた。

恋人たちは優しくなつて歩みながら、
やつぱり、息をつめて待つてゐた。

サキの沼津

空を映してゐるとき、海は
もう真夜中とはちがふ海だ。
きみをおもふとき、ぼくは
雪の焔に身を運ばせる。
海くぐり抜け、
月のきみを
空高く浮かべてやる。

きみの胸が掌に重い。
二人のあひだの百キロの距離は、
綱渡りすべきわが地平線。
夜をこめて
ぼくはそれを端までたどる、
暁方の疲弊のなかで
つひにきみの戸を叩くまで。
テーベーの住むきみの肺の戸。

葉が落ちる。
鳥が高い。

明るくなつた冬ざれの野に
ぼくらの足が道をつくる。
仮眠してゐる苦しみの蟻。
やつらの目覚めを恐れつつ
それでもぼくらはやつらのために
道をつくる、ぼくら自身で。

ごらん、
海が空を映すとき
いつぴきづつの魚の眼玉を
一輪づつの陽がふちどる。
沈みながら、魚は平たい下顎で
岩藻をついばみ
眼をあけたまま眠りこむ。
知らずに深く苦しんでゐる魂のやうに。

わかるかい、

「ぼくは単語にとびこんで
もしそれが、いい言葉だと見極めがつけば、
いつの日か使ふためにとつておくのさ。
長いあひだ『Philogenitive』を暖めてるたが、
あるときたうとうぼくは使つた。

けれどひとつ、最後まで
使ひ途のみつからない単語があつたよ。
"antelucan"
欲しかつたら、君にあげよう。
もうぼくは、こいつについちや
あきらめたのだ。
ミルトン的でありすぎる。」

antelucan
「夜明ケ前」の意味だといふ。

反　歌

ぼくが今まで使つたことのなかつた言葉で

神に入る
箜篌のとほねや
秋曇

愛深くして心狂ふ女らは、
詩を切り裂いて
詩人を遙かに侮蔑する高みに去る者。

ヴィヴィエンヌがそんな女人だつたかどうか、
ぼくの知つたことではないが、
さういふ女のゐることを
畏れつつ、ぼくは知る。

妻の死んだ一年のち
トマスはノーベル文学賞の受賞者だつた。
それから十七年ののち
トマス・スターンズ・エリオットは
テームズ河の一月の霧を曳いて
天空へ去つた。

追悼の記事、評価の文、たくさん彼のあとを追つたが
ぼくは小さなひとつの文を

読んだのみ。
その記者は、エリオット氏との
折々の交遊を語り、
書いてゐた——

千九百三十一年
ヴィヴィエンヌが療養所に入れられてから
千九百四十七年
亡くなるまで、
エリオットは毎週木曜
欠かさず妻を訪れた。
十六年間。
しかし彼女は
この訪問者が何者であるか
最後まで知らなかつた、と。

その記者はまた書いてゐた、
エリオットがある日彼に語つたこと——

倫敦懸崖

ヴィヴィエンヌ・ヘイウッド、
ダンサーだった。

トマス・スターンズ・エリオット、
詩人だった。

二人は、
結婚した。

トマスはまもなく処女詩集
『アルフレッド・プルーフロックの恋歌』を出し、
有名になった。

慎重居士の中年の主人公に
かう言はせたのは大ヒットだった。

「おれはもう何でも全部知つちやつたのだ。何でも全部。
夕暮だって、朝だつて、午後だつて全部知つちやつたのだ、
コーヒーの匙で、おれはおれの一生を測つてしまつた。」

トマスはやがて『荒地』を書いた。
評判は峰を経めぐる稲妻となつて、
野にはためいた。
現代の荒野にたたずみ、
ダンテたらんとトマスはおもつた。

ヴィヴィエンヌは病気になつた。
精神が頽れはじめ
結婚から十六年後
療養所に預けられ
十六年間、そこで生き、
亡くなつた。

病を得た遠因がどこにあつたか
神さまも知つちやゐない。
けれどもぼくは
愛深くして心狂ふといふことあるを、
畏れつつ
心底ふかく信ずる者だ。

Translation on
pages 30–31

調布　IV

三月も末に近い日
家のまはりの土の中から
湧くやうに　蟇（ひきがへる）の群れ出現す。
数十ぴき、
冬眠から
正確に同じ日に醒め、
大柄の雌の背中に
小柄な雄がおんぶをして、
時には上にもう一ぴき、
しがみついてはずるずる落ち
また這ひあがり、
去年までは池があつた
お隣りさんの庭めざしつつ
群れなして、のつたりのつたり集つてくる。
もし池あらば、日も夜も間はぬ幾さかり。
けれど池は消え失せた。
次なる水は森の中。
蟇（ひき）の群れはそれでも愛の讃歌を唱ふ。

姿は鈍、
ちかごろ都に流行の軽蔑ことばで申すなら
オジン、オバンの旅すがた。
だがいざ鳴けば、
アイドル歌手らよ、三舎を避けよ。
太い腹を声をひろびろ反響させて
クワンクワンと、高らかに
朗らかに、大気を顫はす。
ふつうの蛙よ、ギョギョと鳴け。
四、五日のあひだ
昼も夜も空気を顫はせつづけたあと
声はぴたりと四方に止んだ。
いとなみをすませたあとは
夏がくるまで土に眠りにもどるのだ。
人間の眼が浅く地上を掃いてゐる時
蟇（ひき）どもは、そらそこの桜の下にも
丸まつて息づいてゐる。
その上に
花が散つて。

Translation on
pages 27 and 29

詩集《水府　みえないまち》から

調布　I

まちに住んで
まちのことをかんがへる。

住んでゐるこのまちのことは
ふしぎに頭に浮ばない。

いつも別のまちへ
目も思ひ出もよぢれていく。

けれどそれは、別の女を
思ふやうにといふのでもない。

坂のほとり、露草やぺんぺん草に
触つてはだんだん遠くへ移つていく、あの

飛ぶこと自体に溺れてゐる虻のやうに、

雲間にゆらぐまちの塔によろめいたりしながら
いつか、別の空気が渦巻く、別のまちへ

出てしまふ　ぼく。

こどもよ
きみはにんげんだから
石をきづいて生きるときも
忘れるな
土のしたで眠つてゐる虫けらたちの
ときどきぴくりと動く足　夢のながいよだれかけを

かれらだつて夢をみるさ
いろつきの　収穫の夢
おんがくのやうな　水の夢

きみはにんげんだから
忘れるな
植物にきよらかなあまい水を送つてゐるのは
にんげんではなく
くろくしめつた　味のない
土であることを

きみはにんげんなのだから

Translation on
pages 26–27

詩集《春　少女に》から

光のくだもの

きみの胸の半球が　とほい　とほい
海のうへでぼくの手に載つてゐる

おもい　おもい　光でできたくだものよ
臓腑の壁を茨のとげのきみが刺し　きみが這ふ

遠さがきみを　ぼくのなかに溢れさせる
不在がきみを　ぼくの臓腑に住みつかせる

夜半に八万四千の星となつて　夢をつんざき
きみがぼくを通過したとき

ひび割れたガラス越しにぼくは見てゐた　星の八万四千
が
きみをつらぬき　微塵に空へ飛び散らすのを

虫の夢

「ころんで　つちを　なめたときは　まづかつたけど
つちから　うまれる　やさいや　はなには
あまい　つゆの　すいだうかんが
たくさん　はしつて　ゐるんだね」

こどもよ
きみのいふとほりだ
武蔵野のはてに　みろよ
空気はハンカチのやうに揺れてるぢやないか
冬の日ぐれは　土がくろく　深くみえるね
おんがくよりもきらきら跳ねてたテンタウムシ
にごつた水を拭きままはつてゐたミヅスマシ
カミキリムシ
アリヂゴク
みんな静かにかへつてしまつた
土の大きな地下室へ

カンヴァスの余白は輝く

フランシスは　色ある形のうちすぐれて熱く柔らかいも
の
すなはち女の精霊を　雲のすがた　泡のすがた　子宮の
すがたにかかへとる
カンヴァスの余白は輝く

プラスチックとアンモニアの暮しの中で
フランシスの肉体は形而上のオルガスムスに震憾され
しんしんと沈む

ライオンは雷雲に沈み　豪雨の白い歯を剝いて　眠る欲
望の肩に嚙みつく

欲望は不滅への恋
だが永遠は　時の産物にこそ恋をする　とブレイクが囁
く
このとき絵具は　消滅にむかふいのちを燃やして　歓喜

に発光する
フランシスは発光する

カリフォルニアの闇はオレンジの艶を放つ
フランシスの闇は人間の蜜の艶を放つ

絵画は絵画の彼方からの通信だ

フランシスはフランシスの彼方から通信される

彼方の闇は　襲ひかかる牙の歓喜に身をふるはせて
フランシスの絵に嚙みつく

Translation on
pages 23–24

サム・フランシスを夢みる

ある日　めざめると　サミュエル・フランシスは雲の中
にゐた

雲の中から見ると　雲の形はどこにもなかつた
影ひとつない水滴の奔流だけがまはりにあつた
白だけが浮遊してゐた

「形ある行者よ　形なき無上を求めよ　真なるものは形を
もたぬ」と　風がしきりに渦まいて言つた

フランシスは　わが眼の奥から　雲の山がむくりむくり
湧きあがるのを見た

指尖は　帯電もせずにスパークした

「形ある画家よ　形なき霊気をつかめ　雲は形をもたぬ」
と　フランシスの唇がフランシスに言つた
近づいてくるものよりは遠ざかるものに　いつそう豊か

な陰影があつた

フランシスは遠方を馳けた

遠さと近さは動顚し　壮麗な世界の色の環の中で　夕焼
けは朝焼けと結んで闇を抱いた

フランシスの伯父ソクラテスのひげが　禅僧の夢の中で
パチパチまばたきしながら泳ぎ去るのが見える
そのあざやかな一萬の手　そのあざやかな一萬の手

ソクラテスの猛獣めいた哄笑は　ブレイクが鋤で耕す天
空図に衝突し
フランシスは少年の日の火花をあびて立ちつくす

世界は興奮する迷路
波うつ見えない水しぶき
王の墳墓の静寂が　霊気にうたれて切り立つのを　アト
リエの壁は感じ　震へる

石ころの括約筋のふるへ。
石ころの肉の悩みのふるへ。
風のゆらぐにつれ
陽は裏返つて野に溢れ
人は一瞬千里眼をもつ。
風はわたしにささやく。
《この光の麻薬さへあれば
ね、蟷蜋（けら）の水渡りだつて
あなたに見せてあげられるわ》
このいとしい風めが。
嘘つきのひろびろの胸めが。

*

別の風は運んでゐる。
つひにまともな言葉にまで熟さなかつた人語のざわめき
ああいふ人語は
仮死状態だとなぜこんなにもなつかしいのか。

すべての木の葉の繊毛に
こんもり露をもりあげる
気体の規則ただしい夜のいとなみも
かすかなざわめきに満ちてゐるのではないか。
人間は神経細胞（ニューロン）の樹状突起をそよがせて
夜ごとあれらの樹の液と
ざわめきを感応させてゐるのではないか。

そしてたがひのあひだには
もんどりうつて滑走し、あらゆる隙間を埋めることに熱
中する透明な遊行者が
ふかい空間の網を張つてゐるのではないか。

Translation on
pages 19–22

石段に焼きつけられた人の影も
歩きだすのだ　このまちでは
まちぜんたいが焼きつけられているんだよ
宇宙の暗い穴ぼこに

そのまちで
君に逢うかもしれないな
だってそこはぼくたちの
生れ故郷の星なのだから

言ってください　どうか
「おまえは
夢見の
わるい子ね」

詩集《悲歌と祝禱》から

風の説

風には種子も蔕もない。　果実のやうに完結することを知らぬ。

わたしが歩くと、足もとに風が起る。　けれどそれは、たちまち消える溜息だ。　ほんとの風は、かならず遠方に起り、遠方に消える。

風には種子も蔕もない。　果実のやうに熟すことを知らぬ。

風はたえずもんどりうつて滑走し、あらゆる隙間を埋めることに熱中する透明な遊行者だ。

それは空中に位置を移した透明な水といふべきだ。

*

雨後。　浅瀬あり。

林をたどつていく。

色鳥の繁殖。　物音の空へのしろい浸透。

石はせせらぎに灌腸される。

無限の広さと有限の広さを
創造なさり
わずか七日で
すべての仕事を了えられた
それからすべてを
浄められた

地には平和を
人には歓びを

石造りの大きな通りを歩いていったよ
にぶい光りが足もとから射していたんだ
出会ったぼろぼろの帽子の男に
道をきいて進んでいっても
けっして行きつきやしなかったのさ
「あなた　あそこでぼろぼろのチョッキの人に
くわしく道をきいてきたのにみつかりません」
「おや　あなた　その人なら

八年前に流行りやまいでぽくっと逝った
噴水横の床屋のおやじじゃありませんか」
親切におしえてくれたそのひとが
もう五十年もむかし
川に溺れてみまかった地図屋さんだという話なのさ

ところがそれもちがっていてね
ある夏とつぜん
ひとり残らず　一瞬に
このまちへ移っていたのだ
太陽の五万倍の明るさの
光が空でひらめいて
花輪をかざる葬いもない
遊ぶ子供の声もない
みんなあのときのままの姿で
水の中の影のように
こうして歩いているんだよ

あのかたの声が沁みとおった

地には平和を
人には歓びを

たすけてください　どうか
夕陽さえ住もうとしない
骨の森　骨の森にさまよって
青空のかけらをさがし
ちいさな指のかけらを見つけた
ほら
ほら　これが
あれほどにしゃぶりあった
恋人のかたみの小指

あのかたはごじぶんの姿そっくりに
人のかたちをおつくりになった

あのかたは人間を祝いそして言われた

生みなさい
ふやしなさい

アジアの河
ヨーロッパの湖水
アメリカの運河
アフリカの瀧を
人間の皮膚が流れる
むいたキウリの皮のように
顔のないいくつもの国で
顔のないいくつもの手が
血に濡れた金銭をかぞえている

あのかたは無限の時と有限の時

*Translation on
pages 16–19*

いつか、これと似た光景に出会ったことがある、と私は
思った。しかしそれは確かでなかった。

私は叫んだ。

──聞かしてくれ！　あなたの名は？

人垣がどっと笑って崩れていった。

私の耳には、女の囁きも笑いも聞こえなかった。しかし
私は、すべてが天地開闢の日と同じ荘厳さをもってすみや
かに移動しつつあることを感じながら、荒涼たる都市の方
へと歩みはじめている。

言ってください　どうか

あのかたは言われた
水にはいきもの限りなく生れ
鳥は青空のおもて
地の上を限りなく飛べと

あのかたは　巨大なさかなと
限りなく水に湧くすべての生きものを
おのもおのも　似たもの同士のむれとして
おつくりになり
また翼あるすべての鳥を
おのもおのも　似たもの同士のむれとして
おつくりになり

祝福の手を　夜のはてまで
ゆっくりとお振りになった

きらきらとその手先から星がこぼれ
銀河からわたしのあばら家まで

あなたの瞑想をつき抜けて、時間を蒸発させることができますか。

声につづいて、女の顔が、内からの光に照らされる球体となって出現した。それは表面におびただしい微細な影をもつ一個の遊星であった。樹皮をむかれたあとの、青みがかった甘皮のような軽い気体でおおわれたその星は、私の前に漂い、近づき、ふと見えなくなった。六本の脚は、ちりちりと落ちて、他の蟻の曳く餌食となった。黒ダイヤの光沢をもつ私のくびれた胴は、しずかな血管の脈動とともにしだいにふくらみ、毛が体を覆いはじめた。血の色が私を染めた。

私は今、ひとりの人間に変り、激痛の中で叫んでいた。

——なんという大気の鋭角だ! なんという天啓の旅だ! 激烈な抱擁だ!

だが——私はけっして思いちがいをしたのではない——その声は、私の声ではなかった。それは、私の声の中からせりあがってくる、**彼女**の声だった!

——どこにいるのです? あなたはどこに?

答はなかった。しかし私は、私の皮膚の内側に、ぴったりとはりついたものの気配を知っていた。それは薫る岩のように私の中の魚や鳥を眠らせた。私の中に太陽が蜂蜜となって流れた。

——ね、わたしは負のエネルギーだといったでしょう? それは空の巣をはなれる風の幼虫たちの囁きとも聞こえた。私は叫んだ。

——待ってくれ! とどまってくれ! おまえ、美しい瞬間! 狂った美しい女よ!

そのとき、私のまわりには大勢の人間が集まって、にやにや笑いながら私を見つめていた。

私は地上に全裸で立っていた。私のからだには、暁の野の露が一面に浮かんでいた。私は自分のからだを見まわし、肉体がなだらかな丘になって、暁の黄金色の大気の中に溶けこんでいるのを見た。

人々の垣根のむこうには、埃っぽい都市の景観がひろがり、ハイウェーが蛇行し、ビジネスが横たわり、ボードレールの全集の広告の紙がひらひらとビルの壁にはためいていた。

う姿は見えなかった。

──待ってくれ。そうではない。あなたはイメジなのだ！ 詩なのだ！ あなたはたしかに、自己場の中にはいない！ だが、あらゆる輻射の中に含まれる女よ！ 恒常性ある特異性よ！ 生れずに生き、求められずに見つかる、私の影なる本質よ！ 私はあなたに含まれることによってあなたを含む！ 超意味の軌道、裸の薔薇よ！ 私の蜜よ！ 待ってくれ。

そのとき、私は気づいたのだ、私が一匹の蟻に変って、大きな都市のへりをめぐる河っぷちで木の汁を集めているのに！

こうして虫になってみると、世界の大部分は触角でできていることは明らかだった。私の食事は貧しく、私の労働は閉ざされていた。音響は私の触角の向く方向で度はずれに大きく、触角からはずれた領域の音響はいちじるしく覆われていた。そのため私は、われ知らず触角をぐるぐる回転させながら、音の振動と方角をはかっていた。

──おれはレーダーになってしまった。だがこの回転には盲点がある。われとわが身にさまたげられて、この頭、この胴の下だけは触角を向けることができぬ。敵があらわれるなら、おれの体の真下からだ。

私はそのため、たえず位置を移動しつつ、不安にかられて、都市の迷路、台地の露、砂の低地に歩みを移した。私の食事は貧しく、私の労働は閉ざされていた。

──私のうたは電波の裸体よ！

──私のうたは触角の霧箱よ！

草ヒバリめが空中のガラス箱で歌っていた。星が寝返りをうってくるしみ、その血は地上の宝石から光となって洩れていた。おびただしい手が何かをつかもうとして垂直にのび、その先端で互いにはげしく争っていた。破れた指の血は、船の水脈をひいて指の岬を走り抜け、空の蜂の巣にたくわえられていった。だが、空が血の海でなく、蜜の真珠母色の輝きを保っているのは、なんという循環の奇蹟であろう。

空は快活な現象であった。

──あなたは永遠にいたるいつまでたってもあと一分でしかないあと一分を生きているのです。あなたの労働をつき抜けて、時間を蒸発させることができますか。

をもって、空の奥に蜜が流れた。空は蜂の巣から、定められた旅路を追って、四方に散ってゆく輝かしい蜂の卵であった。私はそのあとを追って四方に散った。

エムペドクレスの丘でエムペドクレスが説いていた。「愛と憎しみの力は、火、水、気、土の結合、離反の根源である。このことについて、遠い未来の人類はなおもさまざまな解釈をくりかえし、暗さのなかにとどまるだろう。」しかし、原子は変化することを好まず、ひとつひとつの原子が、「主よ、わがかたわらにいませ、夕されば」という言葉の形に輪になって、互いに寄りそっていた。

非圧縮性の流体が、光の棒に化けて、天の梁に衝突してはとどろきを発していた。そのドラムのリズムにあわせて、雄牛の脛の骨から切りとった笛を吹く女と、荒涼たる湖水の葦原の一本の葦でつくった笛を吹く男が、千キロ離れた二つの岸辺で、世界にはじめてひびく音楽をかなでようとしていた。

すべては天地開闢の日と同じ荘厳さをもってすみやかに移動しつつあった。

――あなたは今、はじめて私の胎内に横たわっています。

でも、私はあなたを生むことはないでしょう。なぜなら、私はもうあなたを生んでしまったのだから。

あの女の声だった。私はいった。

――今さら生れる必要があるでしょうか。私はこの天地開闢の恍惚のなかで充分に生きています！ 自然よ、星が落ちはじめるときの、何とさわやかな朝！

女はくすくす笑った。笑いが彼女を私の目に見えるようにした。美しい年齢不詳の顔が私の前にあらわれた。

――恍惚？ さわやかな朝？

彼女の笑いは私のなかの防腐剤を一瞬にして溶かしたようであった。胸がつまる。その高圧の苦しみのなかで、私はおのれが、腐敗を運命づけられたおのれ自身に幽閉されていることを知った。怒りが波うち、身震いが襲ってきた。

――おお、噴水よ！ それならなぜ……なぜ私は、微細構造常数でわが身がかたちづくられていると感じたのか？ 失われた調和の大陸よ、わが肉のうちなる……

女は私をじっと見つめていた。

――私のエネルギーは、負のエネルギーなの。

女はたしかにそう呟いたようにみえたが、その瞬間、も

——聞かしてくれ！　あなたの名は？

人垣がどっと笑って、崩れていった。

女の声が私の耳もとで囁いた。

——わたしのことを、うたと呼んだ人がいます。遠い古代人ですけれど。近代の人はさまざまに尾ひれをつけてわたしの名を呼んでいます。でも、だれひとり、わたしを《女》にしてくれた人はいない。一緒に寝た人々もいる。けれど、かれらは狂人になり、廃人になり、二度とわたしの《男》になることはできなかった。狂人や廃人は、そうなった瞬間から、わたしの内側に入ってしまうのですもの。ですからいつも、わたしはわたしと同衾することで終る。わたしはいつまでこうして渇いていなければならないのでしょう。詩人などとよばれている人たちは、わたしへの片思いを知っているだけ。わたしの願いは、街でほんとの人との血を流すこと。体重と同じ重さの意味になり、涙と腐敗と汚物を、わがものとすること！

私は自分の名も忘れるほど、私自身の視覚の内側に深く沈んでいた。視覚はたちまち盲目になるが、聴覚は深層でも鋭く開かれているのが感じられた。聴覚は夜の器官であった。私は夜を内部に持つ一個の天体であった。

解体する結膜炎
定量分析をほどこされる鰐の涙
つまづくサンゴ礁
伸縮する地の壁
眠りこむ噴火口
傾斜する春と梅
蒸発する鐘の音
結晶になって逃げてゆく船大工
渦になって逃げてゆく飼育係の口笛
断熱する名前……

つぎつぎに湧きたつ言葉と、言葉が噴き出すイメージとが、一個の形を形成するため波動をつづけていた。それはしだいに、この私自身の形になりはじめていた。

太陽は神々の蜂蜜であった。天地開闢の日と同じ荘厳さ

ました。《死》はもちろんのこと、《これこそ愛》という人もありました。《汚物の山！》と絶句した正直な男もいました。ああ、本当にたくさんの男たちが、世界に対していだいている小さな欲、大きな恐れをこの山の中に見出そうとしたものです。でも、そのすべてを聞きとったのは、このわたしだけ。——さあ、あなたは何と命名なさる、この山に？

女の胸は語る言葉を彼女に抱かれて翔びながら聞いていた。女の胸はひろびろとして深く、私はとつぜん、嫉妬にくるめいて叫んだ。

——あなたはそんなに多くの男どもを、こうして抱きしめ、空を翔んだのですか！

——おや。あなたもわたしに恋してしまったのね。

彼女は私の首筋に、いとしげにくちづけをした。その眼尻には急に深い皺があらわれ、私はますます深く彼女の胸に抱きとられるのを感じた。首筋のくちづけは、氷の針を射されたような寒冷の気を、私の血液に流しこんだ。私は有頂天になって叫んだ。

——あなたは気違いだ。狂女だ。魔女だ！

——かわいそうに。ときどきわたしに本気で恋してしま

う若者がいる。わたしに抱かれて、空を翔んでいるような幻覚をいだく男がいる。わたしにはすべてを見通す力が与えられているけれど、こういう男をどうしてやる力もない。わたしと真実床を共にしたら、かれらは本当の狂人になってしまうのだから。

だが、私は夢中になって叫んだ。

——なんという大気の鋭角だ！ なんという天啓の旅だ！ 激烈な抱擁だ！

そのとき、私のまわりには大勢の人間が集まって、にやにや笑いながら私を見つめていた。

私は地上に全裸で立っていた。私のからだには、暁の野の露が一面に浮かんでいた。私は自分のからだを見まわし、肉体の一角がはげしくいきりたって空間をめざしているのを見た。

人々の垣根のむこうには、埃っぽい都市の景観がひろがり、ハイウェーが蛇行し、ビジネスが横たわり、ボードレールの全集の広告の紙がひらひらとビルの壁にはためいていた。

私は叫んだ。

この軽い、雪のひとひらほどのあなたをごらん。

私は耳もとで風が冷たく痛むのを感じた。高いところを、私は彼女に支えられて翔んでいた。何もない空間に、ひとかたまりの肉のなかの時間となって、私ははかなく浮遊していた。

——ごらんなさい。

彼女の指さすところを見ると、ふかぶかと酔いが渦巻いている空間に、鋭い気配の矢印がつきささり、《快楽》という光の文字が矢の尖端に揺れていた。突如私は、全身に燃えあがる欲情の火照りを感じて、うめいた。

——ね、言葉は行為の現実態なのです。ほら。

指さす彼方に、《知恵》という、影でできた文字が静止していた。私の眼は、暗い冥府の河底から電子頭脳の構造にいたるまでを、一瞬のうちに見渡した。

——知恵と快楽とは、直観の管で通じ合っているのです。

モーツァルトは自分のこれから書く音楽の透明な立体図を、一望のもとに見渡す力をもっていました。あの人には、直観すなわち知恵であり、快楽だったのです。わたしはあの人の脳髄に住んでいたから知っています。直観の能力は、

知恵の裂傷、快楽の裂傷を通って働くのです。——あなた、裂傷を受けるほどの快楽を知っていますか？

私は驚いて声をあげようとしたが、彼女の手はすばやく眼前に静止する《知恵》という文字をかき消していた。私は割れるような頭痛をおぼえたが、それは直観の衝撃とは、まるでちがうものだった。私は涙が皮膚ににじみ出て、凍てつくのを感じた。

——ごらんなさい。

彼女の指さすところには、空間をたえずかきまわすようにして、汚物の山が移動しつづけていた。血液と、腐敗物と、あらゆる兵器の残骸と、人体や動植物の切れっぱしでつくられた荘厳な塔であった。そこには何の矢印も文字もなかった。

——人間たちはみな、この汚物の山に名前をつけたがるのです。汚物には命名欲を刺戟する性質がひそんでいます。おろかな男が、この山を見て、《富の山だ》と叫びました。この男は、自分の属する社会では、大金持で通っていました。別の男は《信仰》といいました。《革命の姿だ、これが》といった男もいましたし《いのちの塔だ》という男もあり

彼女の薫る肉体

または私の出会った狂女

I

水の底で空気がアオミドロにとらえられたまま凍りつい
たとしたら、こんな微光を発するであろうか、と思われる
ような夕暮れ、私はひとりの女に出会った。

女は狂女のようにみえたが、彼女が墓石（はかいし）のそばに近づく
と、石はおのずと誘われて、低声（こごえ）で語りはじめるのだった。
石が語るところによると、女は透視者であり、術者であっ
た。透視力の所有者がすべて狂者の外観を強いられるのは、
久しい以前からのしきたりであったにしても、彼女の若々
しい顔が、四次元の性的魅惑のさざ波にふるえているのは、
痛ましかった。

風は不安を吹き寄せた。

鳥の羽音はあこがれていた。

水はとこしえのいのちと死の、流れて相寄る寝床であっ
た。その同衾のしとねからは、たえず轟音がひびきわたっ
ていた。それは紅葉をも青空をも火焔をも、轟音に変えて
しまう巨大な轆轤であった。

――あなたは意味にすぎないものですか。それとも、大
いなる記号ですか？　答えなさい。

私はその問が狂女からやってきたのか、墓石からやって
きたのか識別する余裕をもたなかったが、気付いたときに
は私の声は答えていた。

――私は記憶の上にかぶされた蓋だ。しかり、私の存在
は掘りかえされるためにある。しかし私は蓋の下から蓋に
なった私を見あげて愕く空気だ。そしてその空気の記憶だ。
私ははたして存在するのか？

――いいえ。あなたは蓋ではない。しかしあなたは記憶
の中に埋没している幼い老人です。あなたは街で血を流さ
ねばなりません。血が争って走り出るとき、全身に痛みの
とげが生えるとき、そのとげの上にあなたがわが身を横た
えるとき、はじめてあなたは、おのれが若い肉塊にほかな
らぬことを知るでしょう。痛みがあなたの言葉となり、涙
があなたの意味となるでしょう。さもなければ、あなたの
言葉は、六〇キロの重ささえ、持たないでしょう。ほら、

Translation on pages 8–9

詩集《遊星の寝返りの下で》から

呪（じゅ）

死者よ　この乾ききった岩石に棲み　そして遙かな樹根に棲め

たとえば色なら　しののめの色　溢れる泪（なみだ）の真珠母色の光沢（つや）となれ

死者よ　二つの凍った極を持つこの遊星の　千の頂きに　同時に棲め

たとえば足なら　ハイエナ　駝鳥　襲うコブラのつむじ風となれ

死者よ　光のとどく限りの涯の　暗黒の淵に去って棲め

たとえば手なら　海に湧く　大渦巻（メエルシュトレエム）　糸を刺す乙女の指のすばやさとなれ

死者よ　足跡を消し　清浄な空の道をたどり　黄金（おうごん）の波に横たわって棲め

たとえば歌なら　はてしない軍旅の歌　恋の歌　永遠の地虫の歌の涼しさとなれ

死者よ　日光（ひかげ）もささぬ沼に棲むわれらを見捨て　舌にひびく果実となって再臨せよ

たとえば息なら　阿吽（あうん）　嬌喘（なまいき）　鬼吹（おにのいき）の浄火となって再臨せよ

再臨せよ　再臨せよ

死者たち

となりのオクラさんの家の前で、いつものようにカンシャク玉を投げつけて逃げる。オクラさんはいつものように髪をざんばらに振りみだし、はだしで家からとび出してくる。《このガキめえ》と私たちを追いかけてくる。今日は光るものを持って追いかけてくる。私は夢中で逃げるうちに、オクラさんが精神分裂病だということを思い出す。精神分裂なら平気だ。オクラさんはぼくを見てもぼくがカンシャク玉の犯人だとはわかるまい、と気がついて、平気な顔をして引返す。オクラさんは庖丁をふりまわしながら、はッはッと息をはずませてやってくる。腰紐から下はだらしなく開いて、臀も股も丸見えである。私は息をつめて、オクラさんの薄汚れた着物にわざと体をすりつけながらすれちがう。オクラさんの眼尻に、もう何年も前から流れているようにみえる涙が、数珠玉に凝固してぶらさがっているのを、私はちらっと見る。そのとき、私の顔がハシブトガラスの顔をしているのが私の眼に映る。賢治くんはどこにもいない。風がぐんぐん世界の容器を冷やしながら吹きすさぶ。森の奥の暗い部屋の中で、水平に翼をのばしたたくさんの灰色の棚から、猛烈ないきおいで黒い埃が横っとびに吹き散

らされてゆく。しかしその部屋の真中に立っている美しい女は、まったく風の脅威にさらされていない。それは彼女の、首筋から乳房にかけてふさふさと垂れている髪が、微動もせず、陽炎となって彼女を包んでいることからわかる。その女が私の女友達の……女であることを私は知っているのだが、彼女の名前がどうしても浮かんでこない。一瞬ごとに彼女の顔は別の顔に変っているのである。

灰色の棚から吹きちぎられて横に飛び去ってゆく埃は、吹雪といってもいいほどで、私はどうしてもその中心に立っている美しい雪女に近づくことができない。そして、鼻の上に手をあて、辛うじて息をつめている私のうしろ姿を前景において、すべてが、深い透視図法の中へと引きこまれていくのが、こちらから切ないほど美しく透けて見える。

（一九七〇年四月十六日の夢）

いてくる。私の名前を呼んでいるのだ。いつのまにか私は走っている。秋吉台の洞窟から垂れている石灰まじりのびちょびちょした雨の中を、私の友人の家にむかって地平線の上を駆け抜ける。しかし友人の顔がどうしてもはっきりと形をなさない。標札に

好事魔多死

と書いてあるので、私はここに棲んでいるのが、むかしむかし私の空想をしばしば強く刺戟した好事魔という魔物の家であることに気づく。しかし私の空想をしばしば刺戟したのはコウズマという魔物だったことを思い出し、さてはさっきから呼ばわっているコウジマオオシのコウジマと、私の知っているコウズマとがどこかで混ざり合ってしまったのだなと慌ろしく思うが、そのとき私はもう、

《ケーンジくーん　ケーンジくーん》

と崩れかけた竹塀ごしに呼んでいる。しばらく呼んでいると、白い雲に乗った一人の少年が、お経の巻物のようなものを両手でくるくるとひらきながら障子の隙間からあらわれる。一度も見たことのない、睡たげな眼をした少年だが、私はすぐにこの少年がケンジという名前であることを思い

出し、

《お父さん、帰ってきた?》

とたずねる。少年の父親はもう十年前からいないのである。どこの戦争なのかは知らない。

《笹の葉っぱが足りなくて困っているんだ。鳥のおなかを磨くには笹の葉っぱがいちばんいいんだよ。とってきてくれる?》と少年がいう。

少年の顔に、私の腕の長さと同じくらいの長さの白いひげが生えている。私の腕といっても、小学生の腕だから、それほど長いものではない。土手で摘むゼンマイの巻き舌をくるりと伸ばした長さとだいたい同じなのである。私はゼンマイやワラビを腕にかかえて、ケンジくんといっしょに、二人の大好きな街角へ行く。かどには煙草屋があって、あがりがまちのすぐ左手には法華経を書いた掛け軸が壁にかかっており、その家のおばあさんが朝晩おつとめをするふかふかした座ぶとんがその前にある。小さな木魚はてっぺんが剥げていて、私はいつもその木魚を学校にもっていってみたいに自慢したいと思う。おばあさんは私の祖母なので、ケンジくんと私はその煙草屋のとなりの内田米店の

たえた。

《バビロンはいま建設中なのに、どうしてもう崩壊してしまったなんておっしゃいますの、あなたは？》と彼女はたずねた。

《でもそれはほんとにたしかなことなんです。安全保障条約が水に流れていくのが見えましたもの》と彼女はこたえた。

彼女がこちらをふりむくと、それはむかし私に小美術館をつくらせてあげると言って、何枚かの美しい石版画をくれ、男のように握手した、精悍な顔だちのドニーズという女の画商だった。髪がむかしながらに黒曜石の貝殻状の断面をみせて黒く輝いている。やっぱりむかしからカツラをつけていたのだな。

『夏』という題名が初号活字の百倍ほどの大きさの立体的に肉の盛りあがった字で印刷されている透明な本を彼女が差しだすので、手にとろうとすると、本の四隅がさらさらと粉になって流れ出してしまう。いぶかしく思い、まじじと彼女の顔をみつめると、それはドニーズではなく私の妻である。

《なんで自転車に乗ったりしているんだい。火焔樹という言葉が君の手の上で震えているではないか》

《近所の子供たちが森で石蹴りをする丸い石が足りないから、空気を丸めているところなの。万国博覧会って、ずいぶん忙しいところなの。みんながインスタント・ラーメンをすすっているんだもの》

《そんなことはないさ。コンスタブルの風景を見たかい？草の露の一滴一滴の中にたくさんのトウスミトンボが舞っていただろう？ トンボの目玉の中に博覧会がすっぽり包まれて、しぼんだフェルト帽のようにアスファルトの裏側を見せていたじゃないか》

そういいながら、私はぐんぐん迫ってくる雲の中に手を入れる。すると放電が起り、非常に快い震動が私の全身につたわってくる。私は上昇気流の柱になっているのに、なぜ人々はにこにこ笑って丘の上にかたまっているのだろう。

タプタプした女の尻が今は非常に整然と駆けている。

《コウジマオシ　コウジマオシ　コウジマオシ》

火の用心の拍子木のように地平線のむこうから声が近づ

*Translation on
pages 3-6*

野のへりを
ゆっくりと旅していたのだ
なぜか
そのいちまいの葉っぱは
ぼくの言葉で
ひっきりなしに
しゃべっていたのだ

透視図法—夏のための

その部屋は妙に柱が多い。森のようにみえる。
回廊がぐるりと周囲をとりまいているのが感じられるが、
私の眼が惹き寄せられてゆくのは周囲ではなく部屋の中心
部なので、いったいどれほどの広がりをもって回廊がめぐっ
ているのか、さだかでない。
部屋のいたるところに水平に翼をひろげている棚がある。
それらは苔むした岩棚の柔らかい呼吸器官で、唇をもって
いる。してみると、この部屋は瀧壺の奥かもしれない。し
かし、棚の上の絨毯は深々とした灰色で、近づいてみると
それはびっしり積った埃である。
埃がこれほど鼠のざわめきに満ちているとは気がつかな
かった、と私は自分が呟くのを感じる。そのとき大きなパ
イプをくわえた小柄な女が、電気エイのしなしなする尻尾
を鞭のようにゆすりながらあらわれた。
《東西南北以外の方角に行きたいのですが、どの美術館の
壁から入っていったらいいのでしょう》と彼女はたずねた。
《それは私の書棚の上から三段目にあります》と彼女はこ

詩集 《透視図法—夏のための》 から

あかつき葉っぱが生きている

なぜか
くだものの内がわへ
涼しい雨足がたっていたのだ
その明け方

葱と豆腐は
香ばしい匂いの粒になって
光と軽さをきそっていたのだ
そしておんなの脱ぎすてた
寝巻の波もまた

冷たい受話器に手をもたれ
砂が光りはじめるのを
見つめていたのだ
鷗も溶けるしずかな
潮の重いあけがた

ひと晩じゅう
眠らなかった者たちに
昨日と今日の境目が
あっただろうか

ふたりは天を容れるほらあなだった
そこに充ちるマンダラの地図だった

それでもおんなは
なぜか
香ばしい森だったのだ
あかつきの奥へ走る
あかつきの光だったのだ

たからかな蒼空の瀧音に
恍惚となったいちまいの
葉っぱを見たのだ
葉っぱはなぜか

– 171 –

Translation on
page xviii

私から産まれたに違ひないこれらの詩篇によつて、
私自身が産みかへされるのを感じてゐる……

エピローグ　調布X　『水府　みえないまち』

原文

『大岡信全詩集』（思潮社・2002 年）および各詩集初版本を底本とし、レイアウトは主に 2 段組とした。

CPSIA information can be obtained
at www.ICGtesting.com
Printed in the USA
LVHW111020261118
598263LV00001B/26/P

9 784902 075953